Journey Through the BIBLE

Dr. Justo González, writer of this study resource, was born in Havana, Cuba, the son of two Methodist ministers. He completed his S.T.B. at Union Theological Seminary in Matanzas, Cuba, then came to the United States to pursue graduate studies in theology. He obtained his Ph.D. in historical theology from Yale University. Since that time, he has held teaching positions at the Evangelical Seminary of Puerto Rico and Candler School of Theology. Although he now teaches on an occasional basis, he is a full-time writer and lecturer.

His books, originally written in either Spanish or English, have been translated into several other languages. He also has written numerous United Methodist curriculum materials as well as materials for other denominations.

JOURNEY THROUGH THE BIBLE: LUKE. An official resource for The United Methodist Church prepared by the General Board of Discipleship through the division of Church School Publications and published by Cokesbury, a division of The United Methodist Publishing House, 201 Eighth Avenue, South, P. O. Box 801, Nashville, TN 37202. Printed in the United States of America. Copyright © 1994 by Cokesbury. All rights reserved.

Scripture quotations in this publication, unless otherwise indicated, are from the New Revised Standard Version of the Bible, copyright © 1989 by the Division of Christian Education of the National Council of the Churches of Christ in the United States of America, and are used by permission. All rights reserved.

For permission to reproduce any material in this publication, call 615-749-6421, or write to Cokesbury, Syndication—Permissions Office, P. O. Box 801, Nashville, TN 37202.

To order copies of this publication, call toll free: 1-800-672-1789. Call Monday–Friday, 7:30–5:00 Central Time or 8:30–4:30 Pacific Time. Use your Cokesbury account, American Express, Visa, Discover, or MasterCard.

Art: Charles Shaw
11 12 13 14 15 — 22 21 20

EDITORIAL TEAM
Debra G. Ball-Kilbourne,
  Editor
Linda H. Leach,
  Assistant Editor
Linda Spicer,
  Adult Section Assistant

DESIGN TEAM
Susan J. Scruggs,
  Design Supervisor,
  Cover Design
Teresa B. Travelstead,
  Layout Designer

ADMINISTRATIVE STAFF
Neil M. Alexander,
  Vice-President,
  Publishing
Duane A. Ewers,
  Editor of Church School
  Publications
Gary L. Ball-Kilbourne,
  Executive Editor of
  Adult Publications

Table of Contents

Volume 11: Luke   by Dr. Justo González

2		INTRODUCTION TO THE SERIES
3	Chapter 1	GOOD NEWS, BAD NEWS
11	Chapter 2	A STUDY IN CONTRASTS
19	Chapter 3	FROM PREACHING TO MEDDLING
27	Chapter 4	THE COST AND THE JOY OF DISCIPLESHIP
35	Chapter 5	A LIFE-GIVING SABBATH
43	Chapter 6	THE PHARISEE AND THE FORGIVEN WOMAN
51	Chapter 7	JESUS HEALS
60	Chapter 8	PREPARING FOR THE FUTURE
68	Chapter 9	THE PARABLE OF THE FIG TREE
76	Chapter 10	LOST AND FOUND
85	Chapter 11	LEARNING FROM A SCOUNDREL
94	Chapter 12	THE CRUCIFIXION
102	Chapter 13	THE WALK TO EMMAUS
110		GLOSSARY
Inside back cover		MAP: PALESTINE IN NEW TESTAMENT TIMES

NTRODUCTION TO THE SERIES

Welcome to JOURNEY THROUGH THE BIBLE!
You are about to embark on an adventure that can change your life.

WHAT TO BRING WITH YOU
Don't worry about packing much for your trip. All you need to bring with you on this journey are
- an openness to God speaking to you in the words of Scripture
- companions to join you on the way, and
- your Bible

ITINERARY
In each session of this volume of JOURNEY THROUGH THE BIBLE, first you will be offered some hints for what to look for as you read the Bible text, and then you will be guided through four "dimensions" of study. Each is intended to help you through a well-rounded appreciation and application of the Bible's words.

HOW TO PREPARE FOR YOUR JOURNEY THROUGH THE BIBLE
Although you will gain much if all you do is show up for Bible study and participate willingly in the session, you can do a few things to gain even more:
- Read in advance the Bible passage mentioned in What to Watch For, using the summaries and hints as you read.
- During your Bible reading, answer the questions in Dimension 1.
- Read the rest of the session in this study book.
- Try a daily discipline of reading the Bible passages suggested in Dimension 4. Note that the Bible texts listed in Dimension 4 do *not* relate to a particular session. But if you continue with this daily discipline, by the end of thirteen weeks, you will have read through *all* of that portion of the Bible covered by this volume.

Studying the Bible is a lifelong project. JOURNEY THROUGH THE BIBLE provides you with a guided tour for a few of the steps along your way. May God be with you on your journey!

> Gary L. Ball-Kilbourne
> Executive Editor, Adult Publications
> Church School Publications

Questions or comments?
Call Curric-U-Phone 1-800-251-8591.

Luke 1:26-45

What to Watch For

This first lesson is both an introduction to the Gospel of Luke and a study of a particular passage. In general, as we read the Gospel of Luke, you may watch for
- The connection between this Gospel and the Book of Acts.
- Luke's interest in all of humankind (for instance, Luke's genealogy in 3:23-38 goes all the way back to Adam, while Matthew's begins with Abraham).
- Luke's interest in women and their role in God's world. (Today's passage deals specifically with this issue, but you will find that there are many more passages in Luke and in Acts.)
- Luke's interest in the poor and the outcasts. In particular, in the passage we are studying, watch for the implications of the story for Mary, an unmarried virgin, and the relationship between Mary and Elizabeth.

Dimension 1:
What Does the Bible Say?

1. What is the relationship between Luke and Acts? (Read Luke 1:1-4 and Acts 1:1-2.)

2. The passage begins "in the sixth month" (1:26). What does that mean? The sixth month of what?

3. How would you characterize Mary's response to the angel's announcement? (Read the passage, and see if you can find different responses as the story unfolds.)

Dimension 2: What Does the Bible Mean?

Our journey through the Bible takes us now to the third book in the New Testament, the Gospel of Luke. In our New Testament, this book is followed by the Gospel of John, and then by Acts. But in fact Luke is the first part of a two-volume sequence that continues in the Book of Acts. (You may wish to compare Luke 1:1-4 with Acts 1:1-2.) The two passages are joined by a common thread: the first (the Gospel) deals with the actions of the Spirit through Jesus and the second (Acts) tells us of the actions of Jesus through the Spirit. This is why the Gospel of Luke mentions the Holy Spirit almost three times as often as does Mark. In Acts there are no less than fifty-seven such references.

A SINGLE WORK IN TWO VOLUMES

Volume 1: The Gospel of Luke
Since many have undertaken to set down an orderly account of the events that have been fulfilled among us, . . . I too decided, after investigating everything carefully from the very first, to write an orderly account for you, most excellent Theophilus (1:1, 3).

Volume 2: The Book of Acts
In the first book, Theophilus, I wrote about all that Jesus did and taught from the beginning . . . (1:2).

Who Wrote the Books?

Who wrote these two books? From very ancient times, Christian authors said that his name was Luke, and that he was the same "Luke, the beloved physician" whom Paul mentioned in Colossians 4:14. More recently, scholars have argued about whether the Gospel of Luke and Acts give any indication that their author was indeed a physician. It really does not matter. What matters is that whoever wrote these two books was a faithful disciple of Jesus and one well acquainted with Paul and his career. Most likely his name was indeed Luke, and he may well have been Paul's "beloved physician." Therefore, throughout this study, we shall continue referring to him as "Luke."

HAVE YOU EVER NOTICED?

Although we often think of Paul as the most prolific writer of the New Testament, that honor in fact corresponds to Luke. In the Bible I am using, Luke and Acts take up sixty-three pages, while the entire body of Pauline letters, from Romans to Philemon, takes up sixty-two pages. Since my New Testament has 243 pages, this means that Luke wrote more than a fourth of the entire New Testament!

Luke was a historian at heart. He made this clear in the prologue to his Gospel, where he declared that his goal was "to write an orderly account," "after investigating everything carefully from the very first" (1:3).

Immediately after his prologue, he gave us the date of the events he was recounting: "in the days of King Herod of Judea" (1:5). Since at that time there was no common system for counting years, dates were usually given in terms of contemporary events, and most commonly by referring to rulers. You will note throughout your reading of Luke's two books that, as a good historian, Luke was concerned with placing his narrative within its wider context of world history.

Luke wrote his two books about the year A.D. 80. These were difficult times for the Christian church. About fifteen years earlier, Emperor Nero had unleashed the first official

5

persecution of Christians by the Roman Empire. Christians had been blamed for the burning of Rome, and had themselves been burned as torches to provide light and amusement to the Roman populace. Although few among the better informed gave credence to Nero's accusations, and Nero himself was soon overthrown, this did not mean that there was any sympathy for Christians in official circles.

Things got worse as growing Jewish nationalism and increased oppression on the part of the Romans led to rebellion in Judea. Christians claimed to follow a man who was "of the line of David," and therefore could be accused of promoting this rebellious Jewish nationalism. In the year A.D. 62, James, the brother of Jesus, had been killed, apparently at the instigation of the Sadducees, who were the pro-Roman aristocracy in Judea. Then the Roman legions invaded Palestine and destroyed much of Jerusalem, including its Temple. As a result, Romans and Jews alike looked askance at Christians. Thus, when Luke began writing his Gospel, he was addressing a community constantly at risk and in turmoil.

What Sort of Good News Is This?

In that context, what sense can one make of the good news of Jesus? What sort of good news is this, that resulted in exile and persecution? It certainly is not the sort of good news that solves all our problems. On the contrary, it is the sort of good news that from a different perspective may be seen as bad news—in other words, costly good news. It is good news that may require one to live at odds with the rest of society, or even with the powerful Roman Empire. Yet (and this was Luke's overriding point),

---

HAVE YOU EVER NOTICED?

In the Gospel of Luke, the first person to hear the good news of the coming of Jesus is a woman; the first people to hear the good news of his resurrection are also women. Luke is the only Gospel that tells us that the early Jesus movement was financed by women (Luke 8:1-3). Also, sometimes Luke seems to have paired the parables and even some of the actions of Jesus so that a story referring to a man is paralleled by one referring to a woman. As you read Luke and Acts, look for these signs of Luke's interest in the role of women in the early church. You may wish to make a list of the women Luke mentions in these two books. You may be surprised at their number and the important roles they play.

it is still good news! When we read the Gospel of Luke from this perspective, we begin to notice things that we could easily overlook otherwise.

Such is the case with the text we will study this week, Luke 1:26-45. Traditionally, the first part of this text, Luke 1:26-38, has been called "the Annunciation," and the second part, Luke 1:39-45, is "the Visitation." For our purposes here, it may be well to use more modern words, and call these episodes "the announcement" and "the visit."

The announcement was exactly that: the announcement to Mary that she would bear a son. But it was more than that. It was also the announcement that the promised good news was finally at hand.

To Mary the good news was not purely good. We are so used to hearing this story told in church and to seeing famous paintings of the Annunciation that we miss much of the drama. Mary was engaged, but not yet married. For a young Jewish woman at that time, to be found to be pregnant while still unmarried meant immediate disgrace. She might well be cast out by her family. She certainly would be shunned by many of her friends and acquaintances. She might even be stoned as an adulteress.

Read Mary's words in that light: "How can this be, since I am a virgin?" (1:34) We often take for granted that Mary was simply expressing wonder at the miracle of the virgin birth. But there is much more to these words. Mary's words can also be read in the sense of "How can you do this to me? How can the loving God of Israel cast me into such a terrible situation and make of me an unwed mother? Does God not care for me? How can this be? Does God not know that I am an unmarried virgin? Have you not said that I have found favor with God? *What kind of favor is this?"*

The angel did not solve Mary's quandary. He simply told her what was to happen, and then added that her relative Elizabeth was also unexpectedly expecting, and "this is the sixth month for her who was said to be barren" (1:36). To Luke's readers, this would not come as a surprise, for in 1:5-24 Luke has already told them the story of Elizabeth, who had finally conceived after a long time of infertility.

The angel's response, however, was a source of strength to Mary, who traveled to the hill country to visit Elizabeth. The two women had much in common. They were relatives, and they were both pregnant. There were also differences. While one was young and unmarried, the other was older and had been unsuccessfully trying to become pregnant for some time. For one, her pregnancy was an interruption in the normal course of life. For the other, her pregnancy was the fulfillment of hopes that she had almost abandoned. Yet Mary found support in her older relative who welcomed her. In the end, Elizabeth's words applied equally to both of them: "And blessed is she who believed that there would be a fulfillment of what was spoken to her by the Lord" (Luke 1:45).

Dimension 3:
What Does the Bible Mean to Us?

Significantly, Luke began his Gospel with a story about two women. Both received unexpected news. In outward content, the news was similar. They were pregnant. Yet, to one of them pregnancy was the answer to many prayers and even a vindication; to the other pregnancy came unexpectedly, and even as an interruption. One had her hopes fulfilled. The other must have rearranged her whole life.

> When God intervenes in our lives, sometimes that intervention fulfills our expectations and brings our hopes to fruition. At other times divine intervention comes as an interruption.

The same is true in our day. When God intervenes in our lives, sometimes that intervention fulfills our expectations and brings our hopes to fruition. At other times divine intervention comes as an interruption.

Two Very Different Students

Think, for instance, of these two cases. In a seminary class I am teaching, two students sit side by side. They have both been called to the ordained ministry. One is rather young. He was a college student when he was called. He was eagerly looking for something that would give meaning to his life. He did not wish to waste his life in something of no consequence. As he looked at various career options, he was frustrated. Then came God's call to ordained ministry. The call was an answer to his prayer, a relief to his anxiety and frustration.

The other is an older student. He had a successful career when he was called. He was buying a beautiful and expensive house. He and his family had all that they needed, and more. They were content. Then came the call. This call implied a radical change in lifestyle. He returned to school. His income has dropped drastically. Yet, he is sure that he was called by God. At first, his wife resisted, and their marriage went through a difficult time that required serious readjustment. To this day, one of his sons has not forgiven him for this drastic decision.

Both of these students were called by God. For one, the response was easy and happy. The other's response mixed joy and pain. Two similar calls. Because they came at different stages in life, they are also two very different calls. Obviously, we cannot say that, because one call proved costly, it was not from God. Nor can we say the opposite, that because the other call was not as costly, it did not come from God.

Does Good News Always Feel Good?

Throughout the Gospel of Luke, we shall find that this contrast is the nature of the good news Luke presents. It is good news that can also appear as bad news. It is good news that can come to fulfil one's highest hopes and aspirations. But it is also a strange sort of good news that can come only with the seemingly bad news that much that one has been hoping and working for has to be left aside.

It is this shattering sort of good news that we find most difficult to hear or preach. Some of us, like Elizabeth, have been hoping and dreaming about something, and the good news is that our hopes and dreams will be fulfilled. Others, like Mary, find that to respond to the good news will require that we realign our lives, that we change our priorities, that we abandon many of our hopes.

The difference is not always apparent. (Remember, for both Elizabeth and Mary the news was that they were pregnant. But that same bit of news had very different implications according to their stage in life.) The difference will have much to do with who we are, what our hope and our achievements have been, and many other circumstances in life.

What, then, are we to do, especially when the good news does not sound so good? How and where can we find support to make the difficult decisions that are required of us? How can we avoid our tendency to hear only the good news we like and not to hear the good news that sounds to us like bad news?

Finding Support in the Community of Faith

Luke's answer is that we find that support in the community of faith. We will see that especially in his second volume, the Book of Acts. We see it also right here, at the beginning of his Gospel, where Mary went to find support in her relative Elizabeth. The angel's answer to Mary's perplexity was simply that her relative was also pregnant. Mary found support for her early pregnancy in the company of this older woman who was going through a similar experience, although in very different circumstances.

The good news that Luke wrote about is not easy good news. On the contrary, it is demanding good news. As we read this Gospel, we shall find people called to leave their possessions and even their loved ones. We shall find people who could not hear the good news because to them it sounded too much like bad news. We shall find that even Jesus himself had to face some very difficult circumstances.

Luke knew that such good news would be difficult to hear. Precisely for that reason he did not expect us to hear it alone. He expected us to hear and live out the good news in the community of faith. That was why he went on to write the Book of Acts, which tells how that community grew, and how they supported each other.

This study of the Gospel of Luke is undertaken as a community. As you study this Gospel, remember that it is not only a word to you alone, but also to those others who will be studying with you. It is a study that will be valuable to the degree to which you support and guide each other through the questions and challenges that Luke will pose to you.

Without such a community, we shall all be tempted to confuse the good news with whatever we like. We shall be unable to hear the good news when it comes to us in the guise of a costly demand. With such a community, we shall be better able to rejoice when the good news is pleasant and to be faithful when it is costly.

Dimension 4: A Daily Bible Journey Plan

Day 1: Luke 1:1-25
Day 2: Luke 1:26-38
Day 3: Luke 1:39-55
Day 4: Luke 1:56-66
Day 5: Luke 1:67-80
Day 6: Luke 2:1-7
Day 7: Luke 2:8-20

2
Luke 2:1-20
A Study in Contrasts

What to Watch For

Historians are particularly interested in placing their narratives in the proper setting, both in time (chronology) and in space (geography). Luke wanted to make sure that his readers knew when and where his story took place. Therefore, in reading this passage, watch for the clues that would have helped a reader back in the year A.D. 80 to place these events in their proper setting:
- Names of rulers. In ancient times, this was a common method for dating events.
- Names of places.

In this particular passage, watch the interplay of power and powerlessness, of the great and the small, of fear and joy.

Dimension 1:
What Does the Bible Say?

1. If someone had asked Luke when all of this happened, what do you think he would have said? In other words, how does he date his story? (Read Luke 2:1-2.)

2. Why did Joseph have to go to Bethlehem? (Read verses 4-5.)

3. How did the shepherds react? Fear? Joy? Action? Wonder? Praise? (As you read the passage, make a list of their various responses, and how they follow each other.)

Dimension 2: What Does the Bible Mean?

This is a very well-known story. We have heard it since we were children, and many of us have enacted it in pageants or plays. Therefore, it is important that we try to read the story afresh. Imagine how it would sound if you had never heard it before. In particular, note the jarring contrasts that we often miss precisely because we already "know" the story.

A Story of Contrasts

The first contrast appears at the very opening of the chapter. In the previous chapter, we read about a relatively obscure family in Judea. Now, suddenly, we are reminded of wider horizons. "A decree went out from Emperor Augustus that all the world should be registered" (2:1). If it were today, we would say that, after focusing on Judea, the lens has zoomed back to encompass the entire Roman Empire. This was an empire so vast that Luke felt justified in declaring that Augustus's edict applied to "all the world." (What Luke wrote in Greek was the *oikoumene*, that is all the inhabited world.) From "the hill country" of Judea, we have suddenly zoomed back to "all the world." And the lowly story of two women of modest means suddenly became part of world events.

Place yourself at the point in time when Luke was writing his Gospel (around the year A.D. 80). The next emperor after Augustus, Tiberius, had been rather weak. Then came Caligula, Claudius, and Nero. After Nero things got worse: in the year A.D. 69, there were four different emperors. From that perspective, Augustus was the most powerful man who ever lived. To a relatively poor and obscure Christian community hearing the reading of this text, the mention of Augustus right after Mary and Elizabeth must have been quite jarring!

The reference to Augustus and to Quirinius, governor of Syria, was a way of dating the events. (Read, for instance, Isaiah 6:1, where the vision of Isaiah was dated on the basis of the death of King Uzziah.) But it was much more than that. Luke wove together the rule of Augustus with the story of Mary, which he has been telling us. Augustus decreed "that all the world should be registered." And this decree had a direct impact on the life of Mary and her family. Augustus was not just part of the background. Even though he did not know it, he was an active participant in the unfolding story.

Luke, more than any other Gospel writer, was aware of the manner in which "secular" events and interests affected the lives of believers. We shall see that again and again as we study his two volumes. Here he tells us that a decree, issued by Emperor Augustus with other ends in mind, had the direct result of bringing Mary and Joseph to Bethlehem.

> Mary traveled from Nazareth to the hill country of her own accord in order to see her relative Elizabeth. But she traveled to Bethlehem as a result of political forces impinging on her life.

The Powerful and the Powerless

What Augustus had decreed was "that all the world should be registered." Other translations speak of a "census." This was in fact what was taking place: a vast census that included not only people but also animals and all sorts of property. The purpose of such a census was primarily taxation. In order to know how much to tax each province, the government needed a fairly clear idea of how rich or poor the province was. In order to tax an individual, the government also needed to know how much wealth that person had. Therefore, a census was not a very welcome event, for it would probably lead to higher taxes and greater misery.

There was another reason that made a census unwelcome: people had to register, not where they lived, but where their family registered. This obviously proved disruptive. In the case of Joseph, "because he was descended from the house and family of David" (2:4), he had to register in Bethlehem, David's city. Under such circumstances it is not surprising that Luke told us that "there was no place for them in the inn" (2:7). The number of travelers must have been exceptional, far beyond the capacity of local inns.

The fact that Joseph "was descended from the house and family of David" brings in an added dimension. We have heard of Mary, a young woman from Nazareth. And we have heard of Augustus, the most powerful man of his time. Now we hear of Joseph, a descendant of the Great King, a member of Israel's royal family, in such strait circumstances that his betrothed has to give birth outdoors, and the child has to be laid in a manger. Luke had a flair for such contrasts: the powerless maiden, the powerful emperor, and the powerless descendant of a once powerful royal house.

Consider the Shepherds

At this point the shepherds came into the story. They were "keeping watch" over their flock—not, as we often depict them in our Christmas pageants, sleeping by a fire. "Then an angel of the Lord stood before them, and the glory of the Lord shone around them, and they were terrified" (2:9). We have heard the story so often that we find it difficult to understand why the shepherds would be terrified. Read the story in its own setting, however, and other dimensions come to light.

The census and all its implications are the background, not only of the family's coming to Bethlehem, but also of the story about the shepherds. It was at times such as this that the various peoples who were ruled by the Roman Empire felt most alienated from their rulers. A census meant greater taxes; and, because of the way in which they were collected, taxes meant greater exploitation and suffering. In that setting, one may well imagine the shepherds unhappy, and even grumbling, about the census and Roman rule. One can even imagine stories being passed as to how a particular shepherd managed to have his flock undercounted. Suddenly, an unknown personage appears from nowhere, and a bright light shines around them. No wonder they were terrified! Once again there is a contrast that we often fail to see: the contrast between the calm night and the sudden appearance of the angel and "the glory of the Lord."

Between Fear and Joy

The angel's words bring into play still another contrast: that between fear and joy. "Do not be afraid; for see—I am bringing you good news of great joy . . . " (2:10). The shepherds were terrified because they expected the worst. Perhaps they feared that the angel might be a government agent. Perhaps they feared the judgment of God. In any case, one thing is certain: they were terrified. But the angel told them that, instead of fear, they should feel joy.

The basis for that joy was the good news that the angel brought: that a

Savior, Messiah, and Lord had been born in Bethlehem. This good news was "for all the people." Given the situation, and the traditional meaning of terms such as *savior* and *messiah* in the Old Testament, the shepherds would have understood that the one who was born would be the great Liberator whom their people expected.

The mention of "the city of David," or Bethlehem, brings to mind another contrast—one that the prophet Micah had already noted: out of Bethlehem, "one of the little clans of Judah," would come "one who is to rule in Israel" (Micah 5:2). When we sing "O Little Town of Bethlehem," we are not singing romantically about a quiet little town. We are actually pointing to the striking contrast between the insignificance of Bethlehem itself and the great events that took place there.

The shepherds responded, not only with a change of attitude, but also with an action. They decided to go to Bethlehem to see what the angel told them would be there. The action led to confirmation of what the angel told them, and then to further action: "they made known what had been told them" (2:17). Apparently, verses 17 and 18 refer to what the shepherds did while they were still in Bethlehem, and verse 20 refers to what they did after their return to their own neighborhood. In both cases, they proclaimed the good news that they had first heard and then seen. Those who heard were "amazed." Note, however, that Luke does not give us the impression that this good news was proclaimed so widely that everyone heard. Today, we find this perplexing. But all we have to do is remember the political conditions under which Israel lived, and we shall understand that this good news, amazing though it is, must be shared carefully. (You may wish to compare this with what happens in Matthew 2, where the wise men shared the news indiscriminately, leading to the massacre of the innocents and the flight into Egypt.)

In between these two verses stands verse 19, almost as a parenthesis: "But Mary treasured all these words and pondered them in her heart." Often they are taken as merely indicating how proud Mary must have been at having such a child. But they probably mean more than that. Probably, they refer both to Mary's pride and to her insight that all of this would eventually lead to trouble. She "treasured," and she "pondered." The gospel is good news; but it is not cheap good news. It is costly good news. It is, as we saw last week, good news that often comes wrapped in bad news.

Dimension 3:
What Does the Bible Mean to Us?

As we ask this question, the first thing we must remember is that "us" does not refer only to those of us who are gathered for this particular study. Nor does it mean only those of us who belong to our own denomination or who live in one country. It refers rather to all of us who, in various parts of the world, seek to be obedient to God's Word. It includes United Methodists in Kansas as well as Christians in China, Mexico, Fiji, and Sri Lanka. It includes those who are fairly well-to-do, and it includes those who are homeless and who do not know when they shall have their next meal.

A World of Contrasts

It is in this context that we ask: What does the Bible mean to us? In this context the very first thing we note is that Luke's world was full of contrasts, and so is ours. Luke moved from the hills of Judea to the imperial edicts of Augustus, and then back to the little town of Bethlehem. In our world, as we read the newspaper this morning, or as we listened to the news, we moved from the White House to inner city slums, and from the halls of power and abundance to stories of hunger and want. Such is our world. And such was also Luke's world.

Had I lived at the time when Augustus ruled in Rome, I would have expected the most important events in my lifetime to come from Rome. After all, Rome's legions had no rival in the battlefield, and her navies controlled the Mediterranean—which the Romans were justified in calling "our sea."

I would have been mistaken. What Luke said, and what later events have proven, was that the most important events were taking place, not in Rome, but in the "little town of Bethlehem." From a purely human perspective, the center of the action was at Rome. From God's perspective, the center of the action was at the periphery, in unimportant Bethlehem.

Some of our newspapers publish news about Christmas as if it were happening today. If these journalists had been living at the time, do you think they would choose the same headlines? Or would they be writing about Augustus and his census? Would

they write about the babe in the manger, or about the flow of visitors and what that happening would do for the economy?

A Change of Perspective

This perspective is central to Luke's Gospel and to the Book of Acts. What Luke is saying in these two books is that God has acted and continues acting in human history. And he is saying also that in order to perceive this action and to become part of it, we need a radical change of perspective. The truly important is happening, not in Rome, but in Bethlehem. Later, Jesus will confront the religious and political leaders of his time. In that confrontation, although it might appear that he is the loser, he is in fact the victor. Luke's second volume (Acts) tells of similar confrontations between the emerging community of disciples and the powerful of their time.

For us, the meaning should be clear. We cannot really understand Luke's message—we cannot understand the gospel—unless we too change our perspective. Society believes that success consists in achieving power and money. Luke calls our attention to a baby for whom there was no room at the inn. The media tells us that those who are most famous are most godlike. Luke tells us that this child born in obscurity is God's own child.

A Change of Life

This change of perspective requires also a change in our lives. The shepherds were terrified because they had a particular perspective on events. When the angel gave them the proper perspective, they were able to rejoice. They also took action. They went to the manger; they proclaimed the astonishing good news.

We too are called to change, not only our perspective, but the very way in which we live.

> If it is true that God's most significant action is taking place, not at the centers of human power, but on the periphery, then we must seek to share God's perspective and action. We must imitate this strange God of Luke's, who is pleased to come to us in a manger. We must go to the mangers of today's world. There we will find many for whom there is no room at the inn. And there we will also find God!

During the rest of the week, as you continue meditating on this passage and reading other portions of Luke's Gospel, think about the following questions:
- We have been taught to think in terms of "careers" and to measure success by the decree of advancement in such careers. What would Luke say about that?
- We often think that the best way to make the church more effective is to bring more influential people into it and to give them positions of leadership. What would Luke say about that?
- We often think that the churches that can best serve God are those with big buildings, high budgets, and abundant resources. We even plan our church programs on the basis of that assumption. What would Luke say about that?

Dimension 4:
A Daily Bible Journey Plan

Day 1: Luke 2:21-40
Day 2: Luke 2:41-52
Day 3: Luke 3:1-14
Day 4: Luke 3:15-20
Day 5: Luke 3:21-22
Day 6: Luke 3:23-38
Day 7: Luke 4:1-15

3

Luke 4:16-30

From Preaching to Meddling

What to Watch For

It has been said that this text is like an entire program for Jesus' ministry in the Gospel of Luke. Indeed, early in each of his two volumes, Luke placed an important quotation from the Hebrew Scriptures, and this sets the mood for the entire book. In his Gospel, it is this passage from Isaiah. In Acts, it is the passage from Joel that Peter quoted at Pentecost.

As you read this text, watch for the reaction of the congregation at Nazareth. Ask yourself:
- Did they like what Jesus was saying?
- Did their attitude change along the course of his sermon?
- Why do you think it was so?

These are the themes we shall explore as we study this lesson.

Dimension 1: What Does the Bible Say?

1. The text says that Jesus "came to Nazareth." Where was he coming from? (Review Luke 4:1-15.)

2. Apparently at the beginning, the congregation was quite impressed with Jesus' sermon. What was it about Jesus' sermon that the congregation liked?

3. Toward the end of the passage, they were so angry that they tried to kill him. What could have made them so angry?

Dimension 2: What Does the Bible Mean?

The First Instance of Rejection

This is one of the best-known passages from the Gospel of Luke. Jesus' sermon is often given as an indication of his concern for the poor, the captive, the blind, and the oppressed. When we study the text more carefully, we see it in much more than that. It is also the first instance of the rejection of Jesus and his message that will eventually lead to the cross. (Remember the words of Simeon as Jesus was presented in the Temple, when he said in Luke 2:34 that Jesus was "a sign that will be opposed.")

It all began very well. After having gained a reputation and respect by teaching in the synagogue in other parts of Galilee, Jesus returned to Nazareth. As usual, he went to the synagogue on the sabbath. He stood up to read—whether by invitation or as a volunteer, the text does not say—and received the scroll of the prophet Isaiah. From that scroll he read the words that Luke quoted and sat down to preach. He had become a teacher of some reputation in the neighboring areas of Galilee, and now these people from his own town wanted to hear what he had to say.

> The fact that he sat down did not necessarily mean, as it would today, that he was through. In many ancient cultures it was customary to speak in public while seated, especially if what one was doing was teaching rather than making a speech. That is why, even after he sat down, "the eyes of all in the synagogue were fixed on him" (4:20).

The Scripture Has Been Fulfilled

Jesus began by telling the people the astonishing news that "today this scripture has been fulfilled in your hearing" (4:21). We take for granted that the main reason why his contemporaries rejected Jesus was that he claimed to be the fulfillment of the promises made through the prophets. But no. Here he makes that claim, and still "all spoke well of him and were amazed at the gracious words that came from his mouth" (4:22). They were surprised, yes, and that is why they asked themselves, "Is this not Joseph's son?" (4:22) In other words, they wondered how it could be that this man whom they had known since childhood could be such a teacher, and even claim that in his teaching the Scriptures were being fulfilled. They did not seem to resent it or even to doubt it.

If Jesus had stopped his sermon at that point, it would have been a resounding success. Perhaps some would have been disappointed that he did not perform for them the wonders of Capernaum (see Luke 4:31-40); they would simply have had to wait for another opportunity to see such wonders.

Jesus went on to acknowledge that they expected him to perform miracles, and to declare that he was not about to do it. On the contrary, he told them, he fully expected them to reject him, because "no prophet is accepted in the prophet's hometown" (4:24). Then he went on to quote two Bible stories that were certain to infuriate his listeners.

The Story of Elijah and the Widow

The first is the story of Elijah and the widow of Zarephath (4:25). In order to understand this story, it is necessary to know something about Galilee and its relationship to Judaism. From very ancient times, Galilee had been at the very edges of Israelite territories. When the kingdom was divided after Solomon's death, it became the northern part of the Northern Kingdom of Israel, whose capital was Samaria. Then it was conquered by the Assyrians, and later was successively ruled by the Babylonians, Persians, Macedonians, Egyptians, and Syrians. The result was that Jews from Jerusalem looked down on Galilean Jews, who were considered less pure and orthodox. Probably many shared the view expressed by Nathanael in John 1:46: "Can anything good come out of Nazareth?"

In the highly Hellenized region of Galilee, where there was a large Gentile population, these Jews who gathered at the synagogue must have felt particularly faithful and righteous. It must have been a difficult situation for them, trying to live as Jews in a region with so much foreign influence. And it was made doubly difficult by the attitude of the "real" Jews of Jerusalem, who considered them less than good Jews.

Now their day had finally come. The local boy had made good! He had become a famous teacher in the entire region, and he was now back at his home synagogue. They were proud of him, because he would help restore their pride! Perhaps he would even perform a few wonders, like those he did at

Capernaum. Perhaps Nazareth would become famous! No wonder "the eyes of all in the synagogue were fixed on him" (4:20)! He was such a good preacher! And they had known him since he had been a boy—Joseph's little boy!

However, Jesus did not give them what they wanted. He began by making it clear that he was not about to perform any miracles for their entertainment. He told a couple of stories and applied them in a way that proved quite offensive to his hearers.

> You may wish to read the story in 1 Kings 17:8-24.

So, we come to the story of Elijah and the widow of Zarephath. Jesus did not tell the story in detail, for it was well known to his hearers. All he did was make a crucial and disturbing point: when Elijah went to Zarephath, there was a great famine in the land, and therefore there must have been many hungry widows in Israel. But instead of going to one of these widows, Elijah went to Zarephath in Sidon. What made this story particularly difficult for the congregation in Nazareth to swallow was that Zarephath in Sidon was not even Jewish territory. If Galilee was at the very edge of such territory, Zarephath was well beyond the edge. Yet Jesus says that Elijah did not go to any of the widows in Israel, but only to this widow in pagan Sidon! Elijah bypassed his own people and went to this outsider widow in order to fill her jug of oil and raise her son!

The Story of Naaman and Elisha

The second story makes a similar point. Now the prophet is not Elijah, but Elisha. Again, Jesus made a point that is not in Second Kings, but is quite obvious: "There were also many lepers in Israel in the time of the prophet Elisha, and none of them was cleansed except Naaman the Syrian" (4:27). Syria was even farther away than Zarephath. Furthermore, it was Israel's traditional enemy. It was an enemy at the time of Elisha. And it had recently been an enemy when, under the Maccabees, the Jews had fought for their independence. Yet, Jesus said, it was a Syrian leper, and not one in Israel, that Elisha cleansed!

> Again, you may wish to read the entire story in 2 Kings 5.

Now we can begin to understand why the people at the synagogue were so enraged. Their faithful attendance to the synagogue, even in distant Galilee, was a sign of their eagerness to be true Jews, to be part of the people of God, to be among the chosen. The manner in which the Jews from Jerusalem looked down on them must have been galling to these Jews from Nazareth. In spite of that they would not give up. They would continue claiming their allegiance to Jerusalem and its Temple. They would be Jews, even if the "better" Jews would not claim them. Finally, in Jesus the son of Joseph, they had their own rising teacher who was becoming increasingly popular. Now they would be able to show that their teachers and their faith were as good as any!

Jesus Is Rejected

And then this Jesus, son of Joseph, seemed to turn against them! *Do not think that I am going to do a miracle just because this is my home town*, he said. And he went on: *Do not imagine either that because you are Jews you have an inside track with God. Remember Elijah and the widow from Zarephath in Sidon. Remember Elisha and the leper Naaman from Syria. God has a way of showing special mercy toward outsiders! That is why prophets are not usually prophetic in their own hometowns!*

By now Jesus had "quit preaching and gone to meddling." And the people who just a moment before "were amazed at the gracious words that came from his mouth" (4:22) were "filled with rage" (4:28).

They apparently interrupted the service, for "they got up, drove him out of the town" (4:29), and planned to throw him off a cliff when he managed to get away.

The passage is crucial in Luke's Gospel, not only because the text from Isaiah defined Jesus' mission, but also because the reaction of the people who heard his first sermon foretold the manner in which that mission would be received.

Dimension 3:
What Does the Bible Mean to Us?

God Cannot Be Controlled

It is very easy for us to read this story in the Gospel of Luke and to miss entirely what it has to say to us. The way we usually do this is by thinking that this event had to do with the reaction of Jews to Jesus. Needless to say, such an understanding of the text is closely connected with the anti-Semitism that has plagued the entire history of Christianity. It is also a convenient way of disposing of the text. Since we are not Jews, the story does not really concern us. It is simply a bit of historical information that serves to explain why Jesus was crucified.

This is also the reason why, as we hear this story, we often think that the reason why these people were so upset was that Jesus was claiming to be fulfilling the prophecy of Isaiah. The truth is that the text says exactly the opposite: As long as Jesus is saying only that the prophecies are being fulfilled, his listeners are quite content.

The problem is much deeper than that. The problem is rather that we all wish to control and to own God, and that Jesus was saying that God cannot be owned or controlled. The people from Nazareth had ample reason to consider themselves oppressed and marginalized. They were put down, not only by the Roman Empire, but also by their own fellow Jews. Therefore, when they heard that Jesus had come "to bring good news to the poor . . . to proclaim release to the captives . . . and to let the oppressed go free" (4:18), they immediately assumed that **they** were the poor, the captives, the blind, and the oppressed in whose behalf God would act. Jesus told them not to be so sure. God could always find others in whose favor to act. They did not like it!

Every Christian to this day must constantly face the same temptation. We like to think two things, both of them wrong.

Two Wrong Assumptions

First, we imagine that, because we are Christians, God will be especially nice toward us. There are even some preachers who claim that, if you are a Christian, God will give you all kinds of goodies! But even among those of us who do not accept such a crass understanding of religion, we do tend to think that, because we are Christians, because we go to church, and for a number of other reasons, God will show special favor toward us.

That is not true, as the stories of the widow of Zarephath and of Naaman the leper clearly show.

Secondly, we all have a tendency to feel sorry for ourselves and, therefore, to think that when God promises "good news to the poor," or "to let the oppressed go free," that must mean us. To a degree, many of us are justified in this line of thinking. But so were these Galileans from Nazareth, so despised that people used to think that "nothing good can come out of Nazareth." If God was indeed giving good news to the poor and release to the captives, this must certainly be their day! It must be particularly their day, since the messenger whom God had sent was one of their own.

They were wrong. We are wrong when we think along the same lines. While it is true that God favors those whom the world despises, this does not mean that we can own or control God simply by claiming that we are outsiders.

The congregation in Nazareth did not wish to hear that idea expressed. They were ready to be entertained by miracles. They were ready to claim this local boy who had made good. They wished to hear that now they who had traditionally been outsiders were to become the insiders. They were not ready to hear that any who presumed to be insiders—even if they based that presumption on the basis of being outsiders—were by definition outside.

> This idea is perhaps the most difficult to grasp in Luke's presentation of the gospel. What Luke is saying is that the good news is that God favors us. And God favors us, not because we have done something to earn that favor—nor even because we have suffered something to earn it—but because God simply wishes to favor us.

No Inside Track With God

Nor are *we* ready to hear such a thing. We are ready to hear preachers who tell us that Christians are a special sort of folk. We are ready to hear preachers who tell us that, as Christians, we have an inside track with God. We are even ready to hear preachers who tell us that as Christians we must suffer and that our suffering will be rewarded. What would we say to a preacher who came to us and said what Jesus said to his fellow parishioners in Nazareth? What would we say to a preacher who told us that there is no way of having the inside track with God? What would we say if a preacher called us to follow Christ, and at the same time told us not to presume that this gives us any sort of control or ownership over God?

We would probably try to have such a preacher removed, just as the congregation at Nazareth tried to have Jesus killed.

We wish for faith to be a source of security. There certainly is a place for that. Luke's Gospel also emphasizes the other side of the coin: a faith in which you can be too secure is not faith in the God of Israel and of Jesus. It is rather a form of idolatry. The God of the Gospel of Luke is the one who "has scattered the proud in the thoughts of their hearts" (1:51) who "has brought down the powerful from their thrones, and lifted up the lowly" (1:52) and whose "mercy is for those who fear him" (1:50).

This is a message that is difficult for us to hear, but which will come to haunt us again and again as we study the Gospel of Luke.

Dimension 4: A Daily Bible Journey Plan

Day 1: Luke 4:16-30
Day 2: Luke 4:31-44
Day 3: Luke 5:1-16
Day 4: Luke 5:17-32
Day 5: Luke 5:33-39
Day 6: Luke 6:1-19
Day 7: Luke 6:20-26

Luke 5:27-39

4 THE COST AND THE JOY OF DISCIPLESHIP

What to Watch For

Note that the text we are studying has two different parts. Actually, in some of our Bibles it has two different titles: "Jesus Calls Levi" and "The Question About Fasting." Those divisions and titles are helpful, because they give us some idea of the subject of a biblical passage. It is also helpful to read two or three sections together and to try to see the connection. After all, Luke probably did not intend for his readers to read his Gospel in separate portions, but rather as an entire story.

That is what we shall try to do in this study. As you read the passage for this lesson, watch for possible connections between the story of Levi and what Jesus said about putting patches on clothing and about wine and wineskins. It may be that this connection will lead you to insights you would miss otherwise.

Dimension 1: What Does the Bible Say?

As you read the text, look for answers to the following questions:

1. What was Levi's occupation? Was he rich or poor? Was he respected or despised?

2. Who was the guest of honor at Levi's banquet?

3. What were the objections of the Pharisees and their scribes to Jesus' attendance at Levi's banquet?

4. How did Jesus respond to these objections?

Dimension 2: What Does the Bible Mean?

Jesus Meets a Tax Collector

In much of this section in Luke the chronological connection of events is not clear. Luke introduces various episodes with words and phrases such as *once* (5:1, 12); *one day* (5:17); *one sabbath* (6:1); and *on another sabbath* (6:6). This particular passage, however, begins with the phrase *after this* (5:27). What this phrase means is that Luke wished us to read the passage regarding Levi and his banquet as somehow connected with the story of the healing of the paralytic who was lowered through the roof. He wanted us to see that the two were of one piece. In both, Jesus did something extraordinary, and in both, the Pharisees and their supporters objected on the basis of their understanding of the law.

> Luke wished us to read the passage regarding Levi and his banquet as somehow connected with the story of the healing of the paralytic who was lowered through the roof. He wanted us to see that the two were of one piece.

In this particular case, Jesus met a tax collector named Levi (his name is Matthew in the First Gospel—see Matthew 9:9). Levi accepted Jesus' invitation to follow him and left everything behind. Jesus responded by accepting an invitation to a great banquet that Levi then held in Jesus' honor.

Some interpreters have asked: If Levi left everything, how could he still hold a banquet in his house? Some claim that this passage shows that "leaving everything" must not be taken too literally. Others suggest that the feast itself was a farewell banquet. Most likely, the phrase "left everything" was intended to mean both that he left his tax booth and that he also left his occupation as a tax collector to follow Jesus. He obviously put his house and his goods at the service of Jesus, as indicated by the banquet he held.

In any case, many of his guests were his old acquaintances. Luke calls them "tax collectors and others" (5:29), but it is clear from verse 30 that these "others" were people whom the Pharisees would regard as sinners ("tax collectors and sinners"). In this context, "sinners" were any who did not hold to the strictest obedience to the law.

Religious Leaders Object

As could be expected, the Pharisees and scribes objected. Note that they addressed the objection, not to Jesus, but to his disciples.

Their objection was religious in nature. A good religious Jew did not *visit*, much less *eat* with people who were not completely pure (Acts 10:28). So, they asked Jesus' disciples: "Why do you eat and drink with tax collectors and sinners?" (5:30)

At this point Jesus entered the picture. Although the objection was addressed to the disciples, he responded directly. His answer was simple: *a physician must take care of those who are sick, not those who are well*. (Obviously, this passage has nothing to do with preventive medicine. In the first century, physicians were brought in, not to prevent disease, but to cure it.) The implication is clear: Jesus had come to call sinners to repentance, If you are not a sinner, Jesus is not for you. Note that Jesus said that he had come to call sinners to repentance. In other words, if you are a sinner, you must repent.

Now the Pharisees and their supporters raised a different objection: Jesus was not religious enough. The Pharisees themselves, as well as John's disciples, spent much time fasting and praying. Jesus' disciples ate and drank (5:33).

Jesus responded with a number of comparisons. The first had to do with traditional customs at a wedding. He said that, just as people did not fast at the wedding, his disciples did not fast now that "the bridegroom" (meaning himself) was with them. Actually, the words he used were stronger, and the NRSV correctly says "you cannot make" (5:34). The implication is that, in the present situation, the Pharisees and their supporting scribes were about as adroit as someone who walked into a wedding feast and proclaimed a fast.

The time would come when the "bridegroom" would be taken away from them, and then they would indeed fast. Here Jesus announced, as he did throughout the Gospel, that not all was a merry feast. There would also be a time of rejection and pain, when the disciples would be expected to fast.

Jesus Tells a Parable

The second and third comparisons are paired, and have to do with the relationship between the old and the new. Luke introduces these comparisons by saying that Jesus told them "a parable." Obviously, these illustrations are not "a parable" in the same sense in which the good Samaritan is a parable. They are rather a comparison, an analogy, and Luke is using the term *parable* in its widest sense.

The first of these two comparisons has to do with clothing and mending. If someone had an old garment that was torn, said Jesus, it would make no sense to tear a piece from a new garment to patch the old. In that case, one would have a torn new garment, and an old garment with a patch that did not match it.

The other comparison has to do with wine and wineskins. At that time, one of the most common containers for wine was a goatskin sewed in such a way as to become like a bottle. When a skin was new, it was flexible; but as it got older, it became hard and brittle. If one put "new wine"—that is, grape juice that was just beginning to ferment—in a new wineskin, the skin would be able to take the stress as the wine fermented. But if one put the new wine in an old and brittle wineskin, it would not be able to stretch and would burst.

The point is that Jesus' message of the Kingdom was like a new garment, and that he was not about to tear away a piece from it to mend the old garment of the Pharisees. Or, looking at the matter from another angle, the Pharisees wanted Jesus to pour his new wine into their old wineskins—which would not be a very wise thing to do.

The last verse of the passage may appear puzzling at first. It would seem that Jesus was saying that, after all, old wine is better, and that therefore the Pharisees were right. Most likely, however, what we have here is a subtle irony. Jesus was telling the Pharisees that they were so content and self-satisfied with their old wine that they were unable to see the value of the new. (Was he also subtly comparing them to old and inflexible goatskins, incapable of holding the new?) Following the theme that we have already seen several times in Luke, Jesus was making it clear that he did not expect to be generally well received. People were too content with the old wine to taste the new.

Dimension 3:
What Does the Bible Mean to Us?

Apart from Jesus himself, there are three different characters or sets of characters in this story: Levi, the Pharisees, and the disciples. In order to see what the text might mean to us, it will be helpful to look at these three and to try to determine which best fits our situation. (Or, what is more likely, in which ways we are like one of these, and in which ways we are like another.)

Levi

First, let us take Levi. He obviously was rich, or at least well off enough to be able to afford "a great banquet." Most of us are not fabulously rich. In comparison with the vast majority of the world's population, however, we probably are pretty well off.

Levi did not find happiness in his possessions. Perhaps that was because of the manner in which he had gained them, and because he felt the contempt of others. Perhaps it was simply because riches could not make him happy. In any case, in Jesus he found what he needed. And when he did, he "left everything, and followed him."

Why did he feel he had to leave everything? We might think that it was because his riches were not derived from honest work. Why then, did Peter and the rest—who apparently were honest fishermen—also leave everything behind (5:11)?

Most of us **say** that we cannot find happiness in riches. Yet, we are not quite ready to leave them behind nor even to put them in a secondary place in our order of commitments.

Perhaps the reason why Peter, Levi, and the rest felt compelled to leave everything was that they somehow suspected what Jesus later said in this text: that you cannot put new wine in old wineskins. Sometimes, acceptance of the new requires letting go of the old.

Thus, inasmuch as we are like Levi, the text may well mean that we must be ready to leave everything if we are to follow Jesus. Anything "old" that keeps us from accepting the "new" must be set aside, no matter how painful the process. If we are not ready to do that, perhaps we are like those people to whom Jesus referred in verse 39, so drunk with the old wine that we end up rejecting the new.

The Pharisees

Then there were the Pharisees. We are so used to all the negative words about the Pharisees in the Gospels that we tend to think they must have been horrible people. This is not the case. In a way, the Pharisees were the most religious people of their time. It was the Pharisees who were most concerned with obeying the law of God. It was the Pharisees who tried to apply that law to everyday life. They were good people. They were even sincere. The problem was that they were too good for their own good! They were so concerned with keeping every detail of the law, that they had no room nor tolerance for those who sought to serve the Lord, but who were not like they were. All those "others" were "sinners." (Note that when Luke referred to the guests at the banquet, he said "tax collectors and others." But when the Pharisees spoke of them, they said "tax collectors and **sinners**."). They had lost the joy of faith and could not tolerate joy in others!

> Throughout history, Christians have often been tempted by the same attitude. In some circles today, the word *Christian* is used as a self-description by those who would apply to the rest of the world the same sort of standards as the Pharisees applied to the early disciples of Jesus.

There is something of the Pharisee in most of us. Look again at the story. The Pharisees objected to Jesus' eating and drinking with tax collectors and sinners. The problem with bringing Levi in was that after him many others of the same ilk would follow—as the banquet clearly showed. Today, when we speak of bringing into the fellowship of the church those very people whom society rejects and even despises, most of us have difficulties.

Have you ever been at a church meeting where someone has suggested a new ministry of outreach, and others have objected that if we do, the church will be full of *them*? This is probably the main reason why so few churches are doing anything really significant about drug addiction in their own communities. It is safer to keep the sinners and the tax collectors ("publicans") at a distance than to risk being overwhelmed by them and losing our purity and prestige.

The Disciples

Finally, there were the disciples. They were hard pressed by the Pharisees, who asked them why they were not stricter. It is a difficult question to answer, but Jesus came to their rescue. They were committed enough to have left their old lifestyles in order to follow Jesus. Yet, Jesus himself told and showed them that this was no reason to be long-faced, as the Pharisees would have had them be. On the contrary, it was reason to celebrate. Levi did well to throw a party. The disciples did well in attending, and in eating and drinking.

As disciples, we have to learn the fine art of leaving everything that would hinder us, and of being repentant for our sin (see verse 32), and at the same time leading a life of joyous celebration. The "sinners and tax collectors" around and in each of us may resist the call to repentance and may not be willing to "leave everything." The Pharisees in and around each of us may insist that as Christians we ought to be austere and long-faced. Yet the Lord who called Levi, and ate with him, and rebuked the Pharisees, calls us to a repentance and an obedience that leads to genuine joy!

Dimension 4:
A Daily Bible Journey Plan

Day 1: Luke 6:27-36

Day 2: Luke 6:37-49

Day 3: Luke 7:1-17

Day 4: Luke 7:18-35

Day 5: Luke 7:36–8:3

Day 6: Luke 8:4-18

Day 7: Luke 8:19-25

5
Luke 6:1-11

A Life-Giving Sabbath

What to Watch For

As you read this passage, think of it in connection with what we studied last week. This entire section of the Gospel of Luke shows how Jesus clashed with the religious leaders of his time. In last week's lesson, the conflict had to do with the company Jesus and his disciples kept and with their jovial behavior. At that point, what was at stake were general considerations of decency and religiosity. In today's lesson, the focus of the controversy sharpens: the observation of the sabbath.

As you read this passage, try to look at what is taking place from the point of view of the opponents of Jesus. Remember that they were very religious people, and try to understand why they responded to Jesus as they did.

Dimension 1: What Does the Bible Say?

1. In other lessons, we have seen that Luke was very interested in the date of the events he recorded. How did Luke date the two events in this passage? Did Luke claim that they took place in the order in which he told them?

2. If today someone drove past an orchard, stopped, and collected fruit from the field, that would clearly be unlawful. It would be seen as stealing. Is that why the Pharisees objected to the disciples' action? What was the nature of their objection?

3. Finally, look for the Pharisees' action. Were they convinced by Jesus' arguments?

Dimension 2: What Does the Bible Mean?

The Purpose of the Sabbath

Are these passages intended to discredit the Old Testament laws regarding the sabbath? No. Note that Jesus did not say that the sabbath is bad, or that it should be ignored. On the contrary, he accepted the law of the sabbath, and then showed how it could be understood in the wider context of God's purposes and God's love.

It had to be so. According to the Bible, the sabbath was not a human invention. On the contrary, it was a law given by God and based on God's decision to rest after the work of creation. Just as God had rested on the seventh day, so should God's faithful creatures also rest on the seventh day.

Furthermore, the law of the sabbath was originally a very humanitarian law, commanding that a time of rest be set aside, not only for the head of a household but also for servants and animals.

Laws regarding the use of the land were inspired on the same principle, requiring the land to be left fallow every seventh year. This law was so important that, if the people did not obey it, God would send them into exile, and then the land would be able to rest. "Then the land shall enjoy its sabbath years as long as it lies desolate, while you are in the land of your enemies; then the land shall rest, and enjoy its sabbath years" (Leviticus 26:34).

Note also that this law was religious only in the sense that it was based on God's will and God's action in creation. It was not a religious law in the sense that the people were commanded to keep the sabbath as a day for special religious observances. The purpose of the sabbath was *rest*—pure and simple rest. Obviously, as one rested, one would reflect on

God's creation and God's rest and on the joy of a creation where there is a time for joy and relaxation. The purpose of the sabbath, however, was not that one might have opportunity to meditate on religious matters. The purpose was rather that one might imitate God by giving oneself, and all of creation, a time of rest.

> ### A LAW BASED ON THE VERY NATURE OF GOD
>
> "Remember the sabbath day, and keep it holy. Six days you shall labor and do all your work. But the seventh day is a sabbath to the LORD your God; you shall not do any work—you, your son or daughter, your male or female slave, your livestock, or the alien resident in your towns. For in six days the Lord made heaven and earth, the sea, and all that is in them, but rested the seventh day; therefore the LORD blessed the sabbath day and consecrated it" (Exodus 20:8-11).

Sabbath Restrictions

What was originally a day of rest eventually turned into a day of strict religious observances. We can easily understand how this happened. On the one hand, there must have been those who were willing to bend the law just a little. "I didn't quite finish my plowing yesterday. Perhaps I can take a couple of hours this morning and finish it." Or, "That servant is rather lazy. He has taken enough rest during the week. Let him make up for it by working today, while I am enjoying a well-deserved rest." Or, "Jacob, my rival merchant, is selling some of his wares on the sabbath. If I don't do the same, he will take away all my customers." Reasons could always be found to bend the law just a little, and eventually to do away with any rest at all.

Then, there were the religious people who may have initially enjoyed the sabbath as it was intended, as a day of rest and of joy—a day to meditate and to rejoice on God's wonderful love. Eventually, they noticed that there were many who were not taking the sabbath seriously. People could find all sorts of excuses to work on the sabbath, and to turn it into one more day, just like any other. Detailed laws—laws telling people exactly what may be done and what may not be done on the sabbath—were added to diminish the excuses.

Eventually the sabbath became legally complicated, involving concerns such as those found below:

- How far is one allowed to walk on a sabbath? Obviously, one is not

required to remain in bed all day. How much walking is simply necessary, and how much is work?
- Clearly, plowing on the sabbath is against the law. What about dragging a piece of furniture that might make a furrow on the ground?
- Since animals are also supposed to rest on the sabbath, is it permitted to eat an egg that a hen has laid on the sabbath?

What was supposed to be a day of rest became a day of greater complications and restrictions. The people who defended those restrictions were not bad people. On the contrary, they were good religious people who wished to make sure that they obeyed the law fully.

A Case in Point

In the text we are studying, Luke shares two incidents that took place on the sabbath. Luke did not claim that the incidents actually happened in a particular order. He did not say "then," or "the next sabbath." He simply said "one sabbath," and "on another sabbath." At this point, the evangelist was not trying to give us a biography of Jesus, but simply to make it clear that the observance of the sabbath was one of the main reasons for his conflict with the religious leaders of his time. He was also building a crescendo of conflict.

> In last week's passage, the issue was the company Jesus and his disciples kept. In this week's text, the conflict moves to the deeper issue of the interpretation of the law.

It is important to understand that the reason the Pharisees objected to the disciples taking and eating grain from the field was not that they were taking what was not theirs. The laws of Israel were very liberal in this respect, allowing one to eat from another's field, as long as one took only what one would eat: "If you go into your neighbor's vineyard, you may eat your fill of grapes, as many as you wish, but you shall not put any in a container. If you go into your neighbor's standing grain, you may pluck the ears with your hand, but you shall not put a sickle to your neighbor's standing grain" (Deuteronomy 23:24-25).

The problem was not that they were eating someone else's grain. The problem was that they were doing it on the sabbath. They were harvesting on the sabbath, and harvesting on that day was expressly forbidden.

Jesus responded by referring to an ancient story about David. You may wish to read it in 1 Samuel 21:1-6, although the story itself will add little to your understanding of the text in Luke. The point that Jesus made was simply that King David took and ate bread that he was not supposed to eat when he and his companions were hungry.

The comparison with David must have been galling to the Pharisees. How dare this carpenter turned religious teacher compare himself with

the great king? Jesus went even further and declared that "The Son of Man is lord of the sabbath." This is an ambiguous phrase. It could mean simply that humans in general are above the sabbath. The story ends in Mark 2:27-28: "The sabbath was made for humankind, and not humankind for the sabbath; so the Son of Man is lord even of the sabbath." It can also mean that Jesus himself, who often called himself the "Son of man," stood above the law of the sabbath. In that case, Jesus equated himself with God who gave the law. No wonder the Pharisees were incensed!

An Attempt to Discredit Jesus

The other story (Luke 6:6-11) is similar. Tension underscores the plot from the very beginning. Luke told us that the scribes and Pharisees "watched" Jesus to see if he would heal on the sabbath. In verse 9, Jesus turned the tables: "I ask you." In this translation, the contrast is not as clear as in the original. In effect the one who was being observed now put his observers in the limelight. "I ask you." They wondered if Jesus would heal on the sabbath. Now Jesus put them on the spot: What would *they* do if they had a chance to heal on the sabbath? He then looked "around at all of them" (6:10). He made it very obvious that they had no answer, and he proceeded to heal the man.

What was the result? "They were filled with fury and discussed with one another what they might do

> As the plot thickens, the Pharisees were going beyond their earlier attempts to discredit him and were beginning to think about the possibility of a plot to destroy him.

to Jesus" (6:11). They were "filled with fury" because Jesus had (1) seen through their petty thoughts about him; (2) put them on the spot by posing a theological question for which they had no answer; (3) put them to greater shame by doing what they would have been unable to do even if they had been willing—healing the man. Luke made it quite clear that these were the reasons for the enmity of the scribes and Pharisees toward Jesus.

Dimension 3: What Does the Bible Mean to Us?

What About Pitfalls?

As we study this text, the first thing we must realize is that it does not mean that Jesus was against the sabbath. Jesus was against a *legalistic understanding* of the sabbath, which made it oppressive rather than liberating, more like work than like rest.

In our day we may need to be reminded that rest and leisure are a vital part of God's creation and God's plan. Partly because of our own religious and cultural traditions, and partly because of modern-day competition, we are often tempted to work without rest, convincing ourselves that our work serves God. The Bible says that even God rested after creation; we, who are made in God's image, are also intended to rest.

Here again, we must be aware of some of the pitfalls—which were also the pitfalls in the time of Jesus.

- The first pitfall is to turn the day of rest into a day of religious activities. In the Protestant tradition, there has been a tendency to think that Sunday is the same as the day of rest. For many persons Sunday is not a day of rest, but rather a day for different activities. That is not what is meant or intended by the sabbath. A rhythm of work and leisure—a rhythm that allows us to rejoice in God's creation and to restore our strength for further work—is needed.
- Another pitfall is to make our "rest" further work. Our society finds it hard to conceive that there is any value in simply doing nothing. Significantly, we call that "wasting time." Yet real rest is not changing from the frantic activity of work to some other frantic activity. Real rest is *rest*. There is a place for rest. When was the last time you spent a day resting? Perhaps if you did, you would discover new and beautiful dimensions to life.
- Finally, there is the danger that we may make so many rules and regulations about our rest that it will lose its really restful dimension. That was part of the problem with the Pharisees. They were so worried

about keeping the sabbath properly that they could not really keep it.

The Purpose of Rules

Life cannot be lived without rules. Most of our rules, most of the time, serve us well in our attempts to serve God and neighbor. Without rules, life and society would be chaotic. However, we must constantly remember that rules are made for the service of God and God's creatures, and not vice versa.

For example, traffic lights are a necessary part of life in a modern city. Without traffic lights, traffic could not flow. If persons were not attentive to traffic lights, the result would be chaos. So, normally traffic laws are obeyed. But suppose you are driving someone in an emergency to the hospital. It is a matter of life and death. You come to a red light, stop, and see that no one is coming. Do

> Rules—even religious rules—have been made to serve God, humanity, and creation, and not vice versa. The sabbath was made as a day of rest, leisure, and rejoicing. It was made as a day to rejoice in God's creation. It became a day of such meticulous observances that much of its joy and freedom were lost.

OBSERVING THE SABBATH

Three key Old Testament passages establish the special nature of the sabbath, the seventh day of the Hebrew week:
—Genesis 2:2-3, in which God sets apart the seventh day as sacred because God rested after completing the work of Creation;
—Exodus 20:8-11, in which God commands the Hebrews to keep the sabbath day holy and to commemorate God's resting after completing the work of Creation by resting themselves from all work on that day;
—Deuteronomy 5:12-15, in which God commands the Hebrews to keep the sabbath day holy by refraining from all work as a way of remembering their days of slavery in Egypt and God's deliverance of them.

By the time the Jews returned from the Babylonian Exile in the sixth century before Christ, strict observance of the command to refrain from work on the sabbath was one of the distinctive marks of Judaism. By making a point of refraining from all work on the sabbath, Jews could demonstrate their devotion to their God and show that they were different from the Babylonians and all other nations. However, by Jesus' time, rabbis were already debating the circumstances under which a Jew might appropriately break the sanctity of the sabbath in order to preserve life.

you simply wait until the light turns green? Or do you go on to the hospital? If you simply stop and wait, you may have shown great respect for the law, but no great love for the person you are taking to the hospital! Traffic lights are normally obeyed. Still, we need to keep their purpose and authority in perspective and remember that there are higher values than waiting for the light to turn green.

Jesus did not allow the sabbath to stand in the way of his obedience to God, and we would not allow a red light to keep us from taking someone to the emergency room in a hospital. Rules must be obeyed in the larger context of whether or not they serve God and God's purposes for creation.

The danger is that sometimes we are so comfortable following these rules, that we do not see how they are impeding our wider obedience. The Pharisees did not set out to be cruel to the man with the withered hand. They probably did not think that Jesus and his disciples should go hungry just because it was the sabbath. Good rules blinded the Pharisees to the greater goodness to be done around them.

We have some good rules that are like that. For instance, we have the rule that we ought to go to church on Sundays. Can you think of circumstances when that rule should be set aside? Have you ever been faced by such circumstances? At those times, have you felt the support of others in your congregation or disapproval? What has been your attitude toward others in similar circumstances? What can we do to make certain that rules play their proper role?

Dimension 4:
A Daily Bible Journey Plan

Day 1: Luke 8:26-39
Day 2: Luke 8:40-48
Day 3: Luke 8:49-56
Day 4: Luke 9:1-9
Day 5: Luke 9:10-17
Day 6: Luke 9:18-27
Day 7: Luke 9:28-36

6 THE PHARISEE AND THE FORGIVEN WOMAN

Luke 7:36-50

What to Watch For

This story is very similar to others that appear in the Gospels. Later on we shall have opportunity to compare them. This particular story is essentially about two people—a Pharisee and a woman—and their different reactions to Jesus.

Since we know other stories of women anointing Jesus, and since most of what we read in the New Testament regarding the Pharisees is bad, we must be careful to make sure that we read what the text says, and not what we think it says, or what other similar passages say. Therefore, be attentive to the character and attitudes of this particular Pharisee. Also, be very attentive to the woman's actions. Otherwise, you may read into the story much that is not there. Compare the difference between the woman and the Pharisee. What does Jesus say about the difference?

Dimension 1:
What Does the Bible Say?

As you read this passage, ask the following questions:
1. Where does the action take place?

2. What does the text say about this particular Pharisee and his attitude toward Jesus? Is it at all different from the Pharisees we saw last week?

3. What does the text say about the woman and what she did? What does the text not say—for instance, her name—that we think we know from other similar passages in the Gospel?

Dimension 2: What Does the Bible Mean?

Comparing Common Stories

It is very easy to confuse this story with other similar stories in the Gospels and to form a composite story that is not true to any of them. In particular, there is the story of the anointing of Jesus by a woman in Bethany (Matthew 26:6-13; Mark 14:3-9; John 12:1-8). There are a number of similarities (but also some significant differences) between Luke's story and the other story in its three parallel forms. Let us look at them.

- **In Matthew and Mark,** the event took place in Bethany at the home of Simon the Leper.
- An unnamed woman came in with an alabaster jar of costly ointment and anointed Jesus' head.
- There was a protest (Matthew recorded that the disciples were involved in the protest; Mark simply said that "some" protested), followed by a rebuke from Jesus.
- Jesus indicated that this anointing had been a sign of his coming death.
- All four Gospels include stories that have some common details. The details of this story are essentially four: (1) a woman (2) anointed Jesus (3) with perfumed oil; (4) someone objected, and was rebuked. The differences are much more striking!
- **In John**, the story was essentially the same, except it took place at the home of Lazarus, Mary, and Martha (still in Bethany).
- Mary did the anointing.
- Although no "alabaster jar" is mentioned, the perfume, as in Matthew and Mark, was costly.
- The woman anointed Jesus' feet rather than his head.
- It is Judas who protested about the waste and who was rebuked by Jesus, who indicated (as he also did in Matthew and Mark) that this anointing was a sign of his death.

In spite of the difference in detail, it is clear that the story was John's version of the same tradition that appeared in Matthew and Mark. Indeed, in all three the thrust of the story is the same. The woman anointed Jesus with expensive perfume. Someone (the disciples, "some," or Judas) protested that this was a waste. Jesus rebuked the protester(s). The story ended with an announcement of Jesus' death.

A Different Anointing
- **The story in Luke** is very different.
- There was no mention of Bethany—apparently, the event took place in Galilee.
- The host was also called Simon but he was not a leper. He was a Pharisee.
- There was no mention of the cost of the perfume (although, as in Matthew and Mark, its container was made of alabaster).
- The woman anointed Jesus' feet, not his head.
- The one who questioned the woman's actions (and then only inwardly) was a Pharisee.
- There was no mention of the poor, nor of Jesus' death.

What all of this means is that, while the stories in the other three Gospels probably reflect the same event or tradition, **the story in Luke is completely different**. The few points of contact are minor. Therefore, it is important to look at Luke's account on its own, without confusing it with the other stories.

Extending Hospitality
According to Luke, Jesus was at table with a Pharisee. Luke does not tell us that this Pharisee was particularly hostile. On the contrary, the first impression we are given is rather positive. The Pharisee invited Jesus to eat with him. It was only later, when Jesus described the treatment he had received from the Pharisee (whose name we are then told was Simon), that we learn that he had not been particularly courteous or deferential. Apparently the Pharisee was open enough to invite Jesus to eat, but not open enough to extend to him the common courtesies due a guest.

> Apparently the Pharisee was open enough to invite Jesus to eat, but not open enough to extend to him the common courtesies due a guest.

As they were eating, an unnamed woman came in. "She stood behind him at his feet" (30). In order to understand this, it is important to point out that the words translated in verse 36 "took his place at the table" and in verse 37 "was eating" imply that Jesus and the others were reclining at table. This was the Hellenistic manner of eating, in which one would recline on one side with the head at the table and the body pointing away from the table. This explains why the woman can come in and stand at the feet of Jesus while he is eating (which would obviously be impossible had Jesus been sitting at table as we do today).

The Pharisee knew the woman's reputation. He thought that Jesus must not be a true prophet, for he had no idea who this woman was. Jesus showed him not only that he knew who the woman was but also that he knew what Simon was thinking! In a roundabout way, by means of a parable, he told the Pharisee both that his thoughts were known and that the woman had put him to shame.

> The notion that it was Mary Magdalene has no foundation in the text. It probably arose because it is in the next chapter that Luke first mentioned Mary Magdalene. It may also be the result of mixing this story with the one in John, where the woman who anointed Jesus was Mary. But Mary of Bethany was not the same as Mary Magdalene.

The parable is brief. If a creditor forgives two debtors, one whose debt was fifty denarii and another whose debt was five hundred, which of the two will be more grateful? As expected, Simon answered that the one whose debt was larger would be more grateful.

Up to this point, the meaning of the parable is cryptic. Jesus had not even told Simon that he knew what he had been thinking. A series of humiliating comparisons showed that this woman, whom Simon scorned, had taken actions that should put the proud Pharisee to shame. Look at those actions graphically. Jesus said to Simon: "You gave me no water for my feet, but she has bathed my feet with her tears and dried them with her hair. You gave me no kiss [as a sign of welcome], but from the time I came in, she has not stopped kissing my feet. You did not anoint my head with oil [the word in Greek means common olive oil], but she has anointed my feet with ointment [the word means special, perfumed oil]" (44-46).

Who Is This Who Forgives Sins?

In other words, Simon had not performed any of the duties that a good host should have performed. The woman, whom Simon scorned, had done those duties, even though she was not the hostess, and they were not her duty.

Jesus did not say all these things to put Simon to shame for his discourtesy. Rather, he said them to point out that the reason why the woman was so grateful, and Simon was not, was that the woman *knew* that she was a sinner, while Simon was so proud to be a good Pharisee that he did not even recognize *his own need* for forgiveness. It is only at verse 47 that

Jesus finally let Simon know that all this conversation was in response to his secret thought, that Jesus must not be a prophet, since he did not know that the woman was a sinner. Jesus knew that the woman was a sinner. He also knew that she had been forgiven, and that this was the reason why she was acting as she was: "Therefore, I tell you, her sins, which were many, have been forgiven; hence she has shown great love. But the one to whom little is forgiven, loves little" (47).

> The contrast is double: Simon did not think that Jesus' head was good enough for common oil; the woman anointed his feet with special perfumed oil.

What took place in the entire episode was one of those "great reversals" of which Luke was so fond. The Pharisee, who thought he knew what was going on better than Jesus, was shown to have been mistaken. Jesus knew that the woman was a sinner, and also that the Pharisee was thinking that Jesus was not a prophet. The Pharisee, who thought he was playing the host, and playing it in a manner that was humiliating to Jesus, was told that the woman was a better hostess; and he himself was humiliated. The Pharisee, who was proud of his status above the weeping woman, was shown to be not only a sinner but also still standing in need of forgiveness.

Luke did not tell us what the Pharisee's reaction was. Indeed, in verse 48 attention shifts completely to the woman and to what Jesus told her, and the host was simply ignored.

Others like Simon, however, were not ignored. These were "those who were at the table with him," who asked themselves, "Who is this who even forgives sins?" (49)

Dimension 3:
What Does the Bible Mean to Us?

One way to approach a biblical text—especially a narrative such as the one we are now studying—is to try to assume the role of various characters in the same story.

Are We Ready to Receive Jesus?

In this particular case, there are three characters, or groups of characters, who relate in various ways to Jesus and to the events that are taking place: (1) Simon the Pharisee; (2) the other guests at table; (3) the woman with the alabaster jar. For our purposes here, we shall take each character in order, see how he, she, or they related to what was taking place, and see what each has to teach us.

(1) Simon the Pharisee. Luke introduces Simon artfully. All that Luke says at the beginning is that he was a Pharisee and that he had invited Jesus to eat. Later, as the story unfolds, we learn his name. We learn also that, although Simon had indeed invited Jesus, he had his doubts and had not even extended the common courtesies that a guest could expect.

> Having Jesus as a guest can be uncomfortable. If we really allow him to sit at our table, he may ask discomforting questions, just as he did at Simon's table. Are we willing to receive Jesus?

That says much about us. We too are often defined by a position ("she is a lawyer") or by a relationship ("he is Isabella's father") or by a single action ("she invited Mark to dinner") or by belonging to a group ("she is United Methodist"). The fact is that such definitions, useful as they are, say very little as to who we really are. Much more important than such "handles" are our inner thoughts and attitudes, and the actions that express our thoughts and attitudes.

Simon invited Jesus. Apparently he did so out of curiosity, or because he felt compelled to do so. In any case, even though he invited him, he did not really invite Jesus to be an honored guest—much less a teacher, although he gave him that title in the story.

In a way, we too are constantly dining with Jesus. We may pray in his name before every meal, indicating that we believe he is present. In church, every time we take Communion, we are sitting at table with him. Is he really the honored guest he ought to be?

(2) The woman with the alabaster jar. We do not know much about the woman with the alabaster jar. We do not know her name. We know that she was a sinner. Simon knew it, and Jesus agreed with him on that point. Importantly, she was a repentant and forgiven sinner. She showed it in unmistakable and even daring ways. She entered into the house of the Pharisee and touched the Teacher. She could easily have been rebuffed. Actually, one can easily come to the conclusion that the only reason why she was allowed to remain was because Simon was using her to test Jesus. But remain she did. Even though it was not her duty to do so, she extended to Jesus the courtesies that Simon had withheld. She only approached Jesus' feet; and yet she was closer to the Master than those who sat at table with him.

Of all the characters in this story, it is probably this woman with whom we would like to identify. Yet, that is not easy. It is not easy because, as Jesus told Simon, what made this woman's actions so meaningful was that she began by recognizing how much of a sinner she was and how much she had been forgiven.

In other words, to identify with the woman in the story we have to begin by acknowledging our sin. We do this in church all the time, when we read aloud a "Confession of Sins." Is our confession meaningful? Do we really believe that we have been forgiven? Or are we reading the prayer and at the same time feeling smug because we are in church, while so many others are "out there" in sin? It is so easy to fall into Simon's trap!

Once we have acknowledged the depth and enormity of the sin we have been forgiven, we must be willing to express the gratitude that such forgiveness entails. The woman's actions and tears were probably embarrassing in "good" company. Perhaps she should have approached Jesus quietly and told him how much she owed him and how much she loved him. But no. She approached him openly and expressed her gratitude and devotion boldly and clearly.

For a number of reasons, many in our society have learned to be embarrassed to speak about our faith, or to declare how much Jesus means to us. We are told that it is not polite to importune people with our testimony. Yet, when we are silent we ourselves miss much of the joy that goes with expressing gratitude. Can we learn something about this expression of our faith from that woman, despised sinner that she was?

(3) **Finally, there are Simon's guests.** Although they were present throughout the events that are narrated, they were not mentioned until the end, when they expressed curiosity and perhaps puzzlement. "Who is this who even forgives sins?" They are there, but they do not get involved.

Is there any chance that we are like Simon's guests sometimes? We come to the feast—to the presence of the Lord in worship—more with the spirit of curious bystanders than of active participants. We are ready to see, hear, even inquire; but not to respond. We are not ready to get involved.

> In a way, we too are constantly dining with Jesus. We may pray in his name before every meal, indicating that we believe he is present. In church, every time we take Communion, we are sitting at table with him. Is he really the honored guest he ought to be?

This is a question we must ask of ourselves as we advance in this journey through the Bible. Is it simply a journey in which we shall see the sights and enjoy the landscape? Or is it a journey in which we are ready to get involved, to be challenged, to change our lives?

Dimension 4:
A Daily Bible Journey Plan

Day 1: Luke 9:37-48
Day 2: Luke 9:49-62
Day 3: Luke 10:1-24
Day 4: Luke 10:25-42
Day 5: Luke 11:1-13
Day 6: Luke 11:14-26
Day 7: Luke 11:27-36

Luke 8:26-56

7 Jesus Heals

What to Watch For

In this session, we shall study three healing miracles of Jesus. As you read this passage, watch for similarities and differences among the three miracles.

As was said in the introduction to this study book, Luke often pairs stories about men with stories about women. In this session there is a story about a man whom Jesus healed entwined with a story of Jesus healing a woman and resurrecting a girl.

Finally, remember that the context in which all of this took place was a Jewish context. As you read the stories, remember the Jewish religious background, especially what was considered clean and unclean and how religious people ought to relate to unclean people. Remember also that

---

PURITY

The condition of being free from any physical, moral or ritual contamination. In the Hebrew Bible people may contact impurity by contact with a corpse, certain dead animals, the involuntary flow of fluids from the sexual organs... or the eating of prohibited foods. While impure, a person is enjoined from certain actions, primarily contact with the Temple or its religious practices.

(*Harper's Bible Dictionary*, edited by Paul Achtemeier; HarperCollins, 1985; page 843)

uncleanness had practical social consequences. Those who were unclean were often made to live apart from the rest of society.

Dimension 1: What Does the Bible Say?

As you read the text, ask the following questions:
1. What are the similarities and the differences among the three miracles recorded in this text?

2. What would be the attitude of religious folk toward each of the people whom Jesus healed?

3. What are the consequences of the miracle for the person healed and for his or her relationship with others?

Dimension 2: What Does the Bible Mean?

The text includes three stories of healing by Jesus (or, more exactly, two stories of healing and one of raising the dead). The first story, about the Gerasene demoniac, can stand alone. The other two—about the women suffering from hemorrhages and the daughter of Jairus—are sandwiched, so that the story of the woman appears in the middle of the story about the girl and her father. Although different, the three stories have much in common, and therefore they should be studied both separately and together.

The Gerasene Demoniac

Look first at the story of the Gerasene demoniac (Luke 8:26-39). The text begins by saying that "they arrived" (26), because Luke has just told us of the storm on the lake of Galilee. Jesus and his disciples have crossed into Gentile territory. The man who came to meet him is described as having demons. Other elements in his description depict him as seriously antisocial. He was naked. According to verse 29, he was so antisocial that he would run away into the wilderness, even though he was kept under guard and in chains (apparently by his family or by other residents of the town). He lived, not in the house, but "in the tombs" (27). The "country of the Gerasenes" (26) was Gentile territory—that is why, as we learn later on, they raised swine. But Jesus and his disciples were Jews, and to them anyone who had *touched* a grave—much less lived in one—was unclean. It was set forth in the law of God, which also prescribed rites of purification in the event that one inadvertently touched a sepulchre.

RITE OF PURIFICATION

"Whoever in the open field touches one who has been killed by a sword, or who has died naturally, or a human bone, or a grave, shall be unclean seven days. For the unclean they shall take some ashes of the burnt purification offering, and running water shall be added in a vessel; then a clean person shall take hyssop, dip it in the water, and sprinkle it... on whoever touched the bone, the slain, the corpse, or the grave.... Any who are unclean but do not purify themselves, those persons shall be cut off from the assembly" (Numbers 19:16-18, 20).

According to strict religious observance, Jews should have avoided all contact with this man who was not only a Gentile but also lived in and among tombs. Yet, when the man came to Jesus, Jesus did not avoid or shun him.

Luke's account of the conversation between Jesus and the man was fascinating, for Jesus was talking with the man, and yet in reality it was the demons who were speaking through the man. In this regard, you may wish to note that sometimes the pronouns and the verbs used are singular and sometimes plural:
- "What have you to do with me...?" (28)
- "Do not torment me" (28)
- "He said..." (30)
- "They begged him...?" (31)
- "He gave them permission..." (32)
- "The demons came out..." (33)

The demon(s) described itself (themselves) as "legion"—that is, as many.

Notice the tragic irony: the man lived alone, apart from all human habitation and society, because he had a multitude inside! He was divided. He was not whole in any sense of the word.

The demons knew that Jesus had power over them, and therefore begged him not to send them "back into the abyss" (31). According to Hebrew understanding, the "abyss" was like a watery chaos, a deep sea, in which the forces of evil were held captive. Again, note the irony here. Jesus gave the demons permission to enter into a herd of swine, which rushed down a steep bank and was drowned. In other words, they did end up in the watery depths!

The swine herders took the news to the city and the countryside, and people came to find Jesus with the man who had been possessed. The man was clothed and in his right mind. The portent is so great that they reacted with fear and asked Jesus to leave the area. Jesus complied, apparently without any protest or comment. The man wished to go with Jesus. He was told to return to his home and there to tell of what Jesus had done for him.

The Unclean Woman and Jairus's Daughter

The other two stories are entwined. Luke begins telling us about Jairus's daughter, then tells the story of the woman with hemorrhages, and finally returns to Jairus's daughter. The events took place back in Galilee, after Jesus had crossed the lake once more. We are again in Jewish territory, and it was a leader of the synagogue, Jairus by name, who entreated Jesus to come and save his daughter, who was dying. Jesus was going toward Jairus's house, when a particular woman touched him in the midst of a crowd.

In order to understand the full import of this story, we have to remember once again that according to the law such a woman was unclean, and should not have been touched.

CONSIDERING IMPURITY

"If a woman has a discharge of blood for many days, not at the time of her impurity, or if she has a discharge beyond the time of her impurity, all the days of the discharge she shall continue in uncleanness; as in the days of her impurity, she shall be unclean. Every bed on which she lies during all the days of her discharge shall be treated as the bed of her impurity; and everything on which she sits shall be unclean, as in the uncleanness of her impurity. Whoever touches these things shall be unclean, and shall wash his clothes, and bathe in water, and be unclean until the evening" (Leviticus 15:25-27).

Like the Gerasene demoniac, the woman was unclean. She was generally cut off from society. Furthermore, she had been in this condition for twelve years and had spent all her resources seeking a cure to no avail.

All of this makes the theme of "touching" particularly poignant. (Remember the last lesson? Simon the Pharisee thought that Jesus should not allow the woman who was a sinner to touch him.) The woman dared mix in the crowd—which in itself was forbidden, for she ran the risk of rendering all these people unclean, even without their knowledge. In the midst of the crowd, she touched Jesus and was healed.

Jesus knew that he had been touched and that "power" had gone from him. (Hearing him say this, would the woman think that her uncleanness had somehow affected him, and that this was what he meant by saying that he had felt power flowing from him? Quite likely so.) The disciples pointed

> Notice that the power of Jesus was such that the woman was healed, even though Jesus himself had not turned to her, nor acknowledged her need, nor spoken words of healing.

THE LAW OF THE DEAD

According to the law, the dead and the place where they die are unclean, and a good rabbi would never enter such a place. "This is the law when someone dies in a tent: everyone who comes into the tent, and everyone who is in the tent, shall be unclean seven days" (Numbers 19:14).

out the obvious: in the middle of the crowd many were touching Jesus. That was not what he meant, and his insistence convinced the woman that she could not remain hidden. For her to say that Jesus had healed her was also to confess that she had done something that she should not have done: mixing with a crowd when she was unclean. There are here all the elements that could easily lead to hostility and to mob violence. Jesus stepped in, acknowledged the woman's faith, and told her to "Go in peace."

Luke then returns to Jairus and his daughter. By now, however, it was too late. The message arrived that the girl had died. Surprisingly, Jesus insisted that she was really asleep and, taking his three closest disciples (Peter, John, and James) and the girl's parents with him, went to their house.

Jairus, a leader of the synagogue, would know the law. Yet, he raised no objection. Upon arriving at Jairus's home, in an obvious disregard for the law, Jesus took the girl by the hand. He touched a corpse, and corpses were unclean! He told the girl to get up and instructed the family to feed her. Finally, he told them "to tell no one what had happened" (Luke 8:56).

A Comparison of the Stories
- As we compare these stories, note that in one story the person healed was told to go and proclaim what had happened. In another, she was simply told to "go in peace"; and in the last, the girl's relatives were instructed not to tell anyone. (It is interesting to remember that the words "go in peace" are the same that Jesus pronounced over the woman who anointed his feet at the home of Simon the Pharisee.)
- Secondly, note that for various reasons all these people were "unclean." Jesus should have avoided them on religious grounds. He did not. Rather, he rendered them clean.
- Finally, a third important point of contact was that all these people were not only restored to health but also restored to community. The demoniac was clothed and instructed to return to his home. That was the place from which he presumably used to flee when they would tie and chain him, and he would escape. The woman, now no longer with a flow of blood, would no longer be unclean, and could return to family and society. The girl was restored to her family.

Dimension 3:
What Does the Bible Mean to Us?

We may have difficulty dealing with a passage such as that of the Gerasene demoniac. For us, disease is caused by germs, viruses, psychoses, hormones, and the like. With that, we think we have actually explained disease away. When we stop to reflect on disease further, however, we realize that we overestimate what we think we know. Although we know much about how various diseases work, the truth is that illness, death, and suffering are still as mysterious as they were in the first century. We know something of the "how"; the "why" is still an enigma. Thus, let us not be too hasty in discounting passages that speak of demons, as if we really knew how to explain evil in a much better way. Evil is such precisely because it has no final explanation—because we cannot explain it away. It is to that mysterious element of evil that the Bible refers when it speaks of "demons" and the "demonic." Anything that opposes the will of God is demonic. Since God does not will diseases such as cancer, AIDS, or mental illness, in this sense they are all demonic—not, however in the sense that the disease should be demonized, as has been done sometimes.

The Case of the Gerasene
In the particular case of the Gerasene, it is clear that he is mentally ill. No matter how we explain it, mental illness is evil—it is not the result of

the will of God, and in that sense it is demonic, as is every other disease or evil in the world.

In the case of the Gerasene, his illness had caused him to abandon his home and city and to live among the dead. The symbolism is quite powerful. He is many—"legion"—that is, he was divided within himself. He lived in the tombs. He was dead in life. He was alone. He was naked. From the point of view of the Jewish law, he was unclean. He was many, and he was nobody.

> We may not be mentally ill. If there is one disease that affects most of us in today's hectic world, it is that we too are "many." Our life lacks a center. We have many centers, many functions, many identities. Each of these pulls us in a different direction.

Do we need a better description of what it means to be "lost"? We have given the term *lost* such an exclusively religious connotation that most people do not know what we mean by it. A person who is "lost" is being pulled in a dozen different directions and has no compass to guide in a decision.

The demoniac was lost because he was "legion." We are too often lost because we are "legion."

After Jesus healed the man, his fellow citizens found him dressed and "in his right mind" (35). He was no longer "legion," he no longer needed to be alone. His own singlemindedness made it possible to relate to others. When Jesus healed, he also restored to community.

The Case of the Bleeding Woman

Consider again the woman with the flow of blood. Her illness also cut her off from community. In the middle of a crowd, she had to be careful not to be noticed, or people would be angry at her for having touched them.

Even without willing it, Jesus healed her disease. He pronounced her well and told her to go in peace. She had already been restored to health; now he restored her to her community. It was as if he were saying: "Go home. Go home, you who for so long have had to suffer from a disease that has kept you from touching your loved ones." The word that Jesus used, and which the NRSV translates as "made you well," is the same as "saved you." In the New Testament, there is only one word for both healing and saving. Salvation is much more than a spiritual event. It includes the entire human being. Here, the woman had been "saved," not only because she had been healed but also because she had been made clean, once more able to be a full member of society.

The Case of Jairus's Daughter

Finally, look at the story of Jairus's daughter. She was dead. Her family had lost her. She was "lost" in the sense that her family no longer had her; Jesus restored her to her family.

In all three cases the people healed are restored to community—or at least to the possibility of community. If it is true that "salvation" includes healing, it is also true that full healing includes community.

The Case of Persons Today

What this means for us should be obvious. Too often we think that "religion" and "salvation" are purely personal things. Indeed, one of the reasons why it is so difficult for us to speak of our faith is that we have been given the impression that faith is a purely private thing.

That is not the case. Faith is also a communal thing. This is so, not only for the obvious reason that community nurtures faith, but also for the deeper reason that faith brings healing, and a healthy life is life in community.

Jesus calls us to him. That is his offer of salvation. Jesus also calls us to life as a community. That is also part of his offer of salvation.

Notice finally that all three people in these stories were unclean according to the religious law. According to the religious views of the time, all three should have been left alone, as far from "decent" human contact as possible. That is not what Jesus did. At least in the last two cases, we are explicitly told that there was physical contact. In one case, the woman touched Jesus, and he did not object, but rather told her to go in peace. In the case of the daughter of Jairus, Jesus took her hand.

Significantly, in the Gospels, Jesus did his most marvelous works precisely with people such as these whom the rest of society wanted to forget.

Today we do have people on the fringes of society who find themselves in a similar situation. These are not the sort of people we usually meet in church, or whose presence would make us particularly comfortable. Yet, these are precisely the sort of people for whom Jesus showed a marked preference and to whom he is sending us.

Think about them. Who are they in our society and in your town or neighborhood?

Dimension 4:
Daily Bible Journey Plan

> *Day 1:* Luke 11:37-54
> *Day 2:* Luke 12:1-12
> *Day 3:* Luke 12:13-21
> *Day 4:* Luke 12:22-34
> *Day 5:* Luke 12:35-48
> *Day 6:* Luke 12:49-59
> *Day 7:* Luke 13:1-9

8 Luke 12:22-48
Preparing for the Future

What to Watch For

The passage we are studying, Luke 12:22-48, is part of a longer passage that deals generally with possessions. Luke was well aware that people spend quite a bit of time thinking about possessions, gathering possessions, managing possessions, and worrying about possessions. He was also aware that how we deal with this aspect of life is crucial to Christian discipleship.

As you read through the biblical text, look for the three principles that Jesus proposed as the basis for dealing with possessions:

- Ultimately we must derive our security from God, not from possessions.
- All of life is to be lived as those who expect a different future, the reign of God. This includes the management of possessions.
- We are but stewards of possessions, rather than true owners in the strict sense. We shall have to render account of our stewardship.

Dimension 1:
What Does the Bible Say?

As you read the passage in Luke, try to answer these questions:

1. Did Jesus say that things such as food, clothing, and shelter are unimportant? Or are they important in a different way than we usually think?

2. To whom did Jesus address the words you are reading? (You may wish to compare Luke 12:13 and Luke 12:22. Look also at Peter's question in verse 41 and Jesus' answer.)

3. Consider Peter's question, "Lord, are you telling this parable to us or for everyone?" What relevance does the parable have for your life?

Dimension 2:
What Does the Bible Mean?

Do Not Worry

Luke 12:22 is in the middle of a longer passage in which Jesus dealt with possessions and their use. If you look at verse 13, you will see that this discussion was prompted by a man in the crowd who asked Jesus to tell his brother to divide the family inheritance. Jesus refused to become their judge, but used the occasion to denounce greed. He then told the story of the man who decided to build bigger barns for his abundant crop so that he could relax and enjoy life, only to find out that he was to die that very night.

It was after this introduction that Jesus told his disciples (note the change in audience from the crowd to the disciples) that they should not worry about what they would eat, or about their body, what they would wear.

> Observe the rising lily's snowy grace;
> Observe the various vegetable race;
> They neither toil nor spin, but careless grow;
> Yet see how warm they blush! how bright the glow!
> What regal vestments can with them compare?
> What king so shining, and what queen so fair?
>   If ceaseless thus the fowls of heaven he feeds,
> If o'er the fields such lucid robes he spreads;
> Will he not care for you, ye faithless, say?
> Is he unwise? or are ye less than they?
>
> (From "A Paraphrase of the Latter Part of the Sixth Chapter of St. Matthew," by James Thomson; *Chapters Into Verse*, Vol. 2, edited by R. Atwan and L. Wieder, Oxford University Press, 1993; page 85.)

As we read these words, two points must be made clear.

- Jesus was not saying that material concerns are not important. This passage is often misinterpreted as saying that the important things about life are spiritual, and material concerns such as food and clothing are not important. That is not what the passage says. On the contrary, Jesus said that these things are so important that God intuitively knows we need them. Therefore we ought not to be anxious about them. The reason for not being anxious is not that they are unimportant. The reason is rather that they are so important that God automatically takes care of them.

- This is not a romantic tale about birds, lilies, and grass. On the contrary, this is a harshly realistic assessment. Grass is alive today. Tomorrow it is thrown in the oven. What Jesus said is that all life is fragile. In spite of its fragility it continues. Life continues because God takes care of it, not because our worrying somehow saves it or does much to enlarge it. That is the meaning of the assertion that all our worrying is insufficient to "add a single hour to your span of life" (Luke 12:25).

The Solution to Anxiety Is Trust in God

On this basis, verses 32-34 bring that section of the argument to a close. The true solution against anxiety is trust in God. "Do not be afraid, little flock . . . " (32). Furthermore, when faith liberates from fear, one is also free for greater and more radical obedience: "Sell your possessions and give alms. Make purses for yourselves that do not wear out, an unfailing treasure in heaven . . . " (33).

These last verses provide a transition to a slightly different focus on the matter of possessions. Up to this point, the argument has been essentially that, since God knows what we need, we should not be concerned over the necessities of life. Now the argument will shift: as people who expect a particular future, the disciples of Jesus must organize their lives around that expectation.

Be Ready for Jesus to Return

Jesus made this point by means of two brief parables that appear in verses 35-40. Since both parables mention the owner or master of a house, it is easy to read them as one, and thus to confuse their meaning.

The first parable speaks of a master who was away at a wedding feast. His servants did not know when to expect him. Obviously, he would return; the question was when. They stayed awake waiting for him, so as to open the door promptly when he knocked. If he came "during the middle of the night, or near dawn"—that is, if his servants waited for him even when they would have every excuse to be asleep—then they would be considered "blessed" (a word that could also be translated as "fortunate" or "happy").

An interesting reversal takes place in this first short parable. The master "will fasten his belt and have them sit down to eat, and he will come and serve them" (37). In other words, the master would now become a servant of these faithful servants who waited up for him. In Greek, the reversal of roles is clearer. The same word was used for what the servants were to do ("be dressed for action," verse 35) and what the master did ("fasten his belt," verse 37). The image here is that of someone who is wearing a long robe, and hikes it up by means of a belt in order to be ready for action or to be able to move more freely. The passage reminds one of John 13:4, where Jesus "took off his outer robe, and tied a towel around himself" so that he could wash the disciples' feet. In any case, this theme of the serving master appears repeatedly in the Gospels. Luke stated it once more in 22:27: "I am among you as one who serves."

The second parable is very short, for it is encompassed in verse 39. Here again it was a question of the owner of a house. But now the one who came unexpectedly was a thief. What is the point? Just as one must be always on guard, because thieves do

> The fact that the Lord is compared to a thief who comes at night might offend our moral sensibilities. Yet, it is clear that this was an image that made quite an impact on the early church. It appears not only here and in a parallel passage in Matthew 24:43, but also in 1 Thessalonians 5:2, 4, in 2 Peter 3:10, and in Revelation 3:3 and 16:15.

not announce themselves, so must the disciples be always ready for the coming of their Lord.

The meaning of the two short parables is then summarized in verse 40: "You also must be ready, for the Son of Man [the master in the first parable, and the thief in the second] is coming at an unexpected hour."

In verse 41, Peter asked whether Jesus was speaking to everyone, or mainly to the disciples. In a way Luke has already answered that question in verse 22: "He said to his disciples. . . . " Peter's intervention made the point more clearly. Luke often used Peter as a spokesperson for the entire group of disciples. Here, Peter's question gave Jesus the opportunity to point out that those who were closest to him bore a greater responsibility than the rest. Again, Jesus did this by means of a parable. The third parable uses once more the image of a master and his slaves. In this parable, however, there were two kinds of slaves. One was the "manager"—the *oikonomos* or steward. In ancient society, the steward was normally a slave who had been put in charge of administering a household or an estate. Since rich landholders often had more than one property, the owner was often absent. Therefore, the steward had quite a bit of power and authority. The steward could, for instance, buy and sell produce, or assign and supervise the work of the other slaves. Though usually a slave, a steward could even hire and supervise free day-laborers.

In this particular parable, the steward was put in charge of the master's slaves and was responsible for their well-being. If, when the master returned, he found that "that slave,"—the steward—had been faithful, he would "put that one in charge of all his possessions" (44). Note that the image is that of a rich landlord who had many possessions. But if the steward, seeing that the master was absent, took that as an opportunity to abuse the other slaves and to live in debauchery, the master would come unexpectedly and depose him. Furthermore, since this particular slave *knew the master's will and disobeyed it*, acting as if the master would never return, he would "receive a severe beating" (47). In contrast, a slave who *did not really know what the master wished, and acted wrongly*, would receive only a "light beating" (48). Finally, the parable closed with words to the effect that those who had received much had a greater burden of responsibility than those who had received little.

The point is quite clear. Peter wished to know if all that Jesus was saying applied particularly to the inner circle of the disciples. Jesus answered that in a way it did; but that this should not be considered merely a privilege. It was also a responsibility. Precisely because the disciples knew the Master's will, and knew that he would return, they would be punished more severely if they acted as if they did not know.

Dimension 3:
What Does the Bible Mean to Us?

Jesus Was Concerned for the Poor

For some reason, we often miss how much of the Bible has to do with economic matters and with the way possessions are to be managed. Much of the law of Israel had to do with such matters. The prophets attacked economic injustice just as much as they attacked idolatry. They often claimed that the two were closely connected. In the New Testament, we often fail to realize that many of Paul's epistles, which we read only as theological documents or as pastoral advice, were also fundraising letters. When it comes to the teachings of Jesus, what he had to say about possessions and their use is often forgotten. Luke will not allow us to forget.

In his concern for economic matters, Luke was standing on firm ground. The Lord, about whose earthly life he told, had taught along the same lines. Indeed, if there is one point in which all four Gospels are unanimous, it is on Jesus' concern for the poor and those who did not have anyone to defend them.

> Luke repeatedly stressed the place that the poor have in the hearing of the Gospel. Indeed, his book has been called the "Gospel for the Poor." His other book, Acts, tells us much about the economic practices of the early church.

The passage about the lilies of the field and the birds of the air has often been interpreted as if Jesus had taught that economic matters were not important. Yet, as has already been said, the truth is quite contrary. *Jesus said that we should not worry about our own food and clothing, not because they are not important, but rather because they are so important that God will see to them!*

Security Is Not Provided Through Possessions

What Jesus did say, and what the passages we are studying state quite clearly, is that it is silly to attempt to derive security from material possessions. Yet, is that not what most of us do most of the time? When we speak of "security" in our society, is it not economic security that we mean? We seek to ensure our security by a combination of savings, investments, pension funds, and insurance policies.

Does this mean that savings, investments, pensions, and insurance policies are bad, or that they are contrary to the will of God? Certainly not, unless we think that we can base our security on them, or acquire them out of an anxious fear that God will somehow abandon us.

Jesus said that God knows that we need food and clothing. Clearly, God also knows that we need shelter, medical services, and other basic necessities. This means, paradoxically enough, that these things are very important—so important that God is involved in them—and that we are not to be inordinately anxious about them, for such anxiety is a sign that we do not trust God.

Now, all this sounds easy. However, there are many people in our world and in our society who do not have enough to eat or to wear, or who do not have adequate shelter, or who suffer from diseases that could easily be cured if they had the necessary resources.

This poses a serious problem for us. Does this mean that Jesus was wrong, and that God does not really care about people's food, clothing, and shelter? As we all know, it is partially on this basis that many deny the existence or at least the goodness of God, saying that if there were a good God there would be no such evil. Obviously, we have no final and irrefutable answer to that dilemma, for evil is by its very nature mysterious and unexplainable.

There is another level at which the answer may be much clearer. In the passage we are studying, Jesus moved directly into the question of stewardship. He did this because, at least in part, the way in which God intends to feed the hungry, clothe the naked, and provide shelter for the homeless is through the stewardship of the people of God. Think, for instance, about the parable of the master who went away and left a steward in charge. The steward knew the master's will. In this case, Christian stewards knew that God's will was that the hungry be fed. But the master did not return immediately. The steward was tempted to abuse the other slaves and then to "live it up." Is that not what we are often tempted to do? We know the Master's will. We know, for instance, that we are supposed to feed the hungry. Yet we do not do it. We act as if Jesus were not returning, as if we would never have to render an account of our stewardship.

Ours is a strange Master. According to one of the parables we have studied, he is quite ready to serve his own servants. He does not stand on privilege, nor demand unusual service. He does demand strict obedience when it comes to those stewards who somehow have the power to administer the Master's bounty, so as to give all "their allowance of food at the proper time" (42). Those who know what his will is, and still do not obey, will be deposed. Furthermore, they will be beaten. In fact, it would be better for them not to know at all, for if they do what the master does not wish, but do it out of ignorance, their punishment will be slight.

Strangely enough, this might well mean that, *if we intend to be disobedient*, it would be better for us never to hear God's message. To hear the good news is a great and wonderful privilege for which we can be grateful. It is also an awesome responsibility, for "that slave who knew what his master wanted, but did not prepare himself or do what was wanted, will receive a severe beating" (47).

Dimension 4:
A Daily Bible Journey Plan

Day 1: **Luke 13:10-21**
Day 2: **Luke 13:22-30**
Day 3: **Luke 13:31-35**
Day 4: **Luke 14:1-6**
Day 5: **Luke 14:7-14**
Day 6: **Luke 14:15-24**
Day 7: **Luke 14:25-35**

9 — Luke 13:1-9

The Parable of the Fig Tree

What to Watch For

In most of our Bibles, the text we are studying is divided under two different headings. The Bible I am using, for instance, has the heading "Repent or Perish" for verses 1-5, and then "The Parable of the Barren Fig Tree" for verses 6-9. There is a connection between the two. In some way, the parable relates to the story in the first five verses.

The first thing to look for is the connection between the parable and what has gone on before. Does the parable have anything to do with the questions raised earlier about why some seem to suffer more than others?

In this regard, you may note that the parable has no "application" at the end. It does not say to what it refers. Therefore, it makes sense to think that in some way the parable is the continuation of Jesus' response to the issues discussed immediately before.

FIG TREE—

A beautiful shade tree with large palm-shaped leaves, producing pear-shaped fruit. Ripened figs taste sweet. They are an ideal food for travelers and are used medicinally as a poultice on wounds and boils.

(Adapted from *Harper's Bible Dictionary*, page 308.)

Dimension 1:
What Does the Bible Say?

As you read the text, think about the following questions:

1. There is reference to two tragedies. Where did each happen? Who were the victims? Who or what caused them?

2. Is there any phrase or theme that is repeated in the first five verses?

3. If you take that phrase or theme, and think about it as you read the parable, does it help make sense of the parable?

Dimension 2:
What Does the Bible Mean?

Difficult Questions Are Raised

Jesus was on his way to Jerusalem. He had been speaking about what it meant to be a faithful people. In that context, someone told him that Pilate had committed a gruesome crime. He had mingled the blood of a number of Galileans with their sacrifices. In other words, he had killed them just as they were offering their sacrifices to God.

The details of what had taken place are not altogether clear. But several things are clear.

- This terrible crime took place in the Temple in Jerusalem, for this was the place where the Galileans would have come to offer sacrifices to God.

- Precisely because it had taken place in the Temple, it was a most horrible crime. It was not only murder but also sacrilege. One may well surmise that many Jews were reminded of the event, several decades earlier, when Pompey rode his horse into the Holy of Holies. They may also have been reminded of another time, many years earlier, when the Temple was destroyed and the people were led into captivity. Readers today may be reminded of the murder of Becket before the high altar in the cathedral of Canterbury, or more recently, of the murder of Archbishop Oscar Romero under similar circumstances in a church in El Salvador.

- What becomes clear when we read the entirety of the Gospel, is that there was a great deal of animosity on the part of some of the Jewish leaders in Jerusalem toward all Galileans. Indeed, many Jews viewed the Galileans as second-class Jews, as standing somewhere between the true Jews and the heathenish Gentiles.

For all these reasons, those reporting Pilate's crime were raising several questions in one.

- They were raising the question of the reason for such seemingly meaningless suffering.

- They were raising the question of whether good Jews should not be incensed at Pilate and all the Romans. In other words, as in so many other places in the Gospel narrative, they were trying to place Jesus in the difficult position of having to appear either unpatriotic or subversive. If he condemned Pilate's act, he would be accused of inciting rebellion against the Romans. If he played down its importance, his listeners would be outraged at his religious and human insensitivity.

- They were raising the question of the relations between Galileans and other Jews. In telling him of the horrible thing that had happened to these Galileans, they were addressing the commonly held belief among Jews that Galileans were less faithful than other Jews. Perhaps this was the reason why Jesus responded, "Do you think... that these Galileans... were worse sinners than all other Galileans?" (2) Jesus sharpened the question by bringing it closer to home and referring to an incident in Jerusalem. "Those eighteen who were killed when the tower of Siloam fell on them— do you think that they were worse offenders than all the others living in Jerusalem?" (4)

By connecting the death of the eighteen with the death of the Galileans, Jesus was responding to one of the issues raised by the report he had received. He was responding to any anti-Galilean bias by showing that similar things had also happened to good Jews from Jerusalem. He was also posing a more difficult question, because in the case of the Galileans, one could blame Pilate for the tragedy; in the case of the tower, no one was directly to blame.

Jesus carried the matter one step further. He showed that those who asked about the unmerited suffering of the innocent were posing the question in the wrong way. The surprising thing was not that so many died. It was more surprising that so many still lived. If it were a matter of sin, we would all be dead. Twice he says: Unless you repent, you will all likewise perish (3, 5). He illustrated his meaning with a parable.

> The suffering of both Galileans and Jews from Jerusalem posed the difficult, age-old question of why some people suffer and others do not.

The Parable of the Fig Tree

A man had a fig tree planted in his vineyard; he came seeking fruit on it and found none. He said to the vinedresser, "See here! For three years I have come looking for fruit on this fig tree, and still I find none" (7). A conversation ensued. The owner of the vineyard agreed that for one more year the tree would be left to stand. It would receive special care. If at the end of that time it still had not produced fruit, it would be cut down.

What did the parable mean in this context? It clearly meant that those who survived, such as those Galileans who were not killed by Herod or those Jews on whom the tower did not fall, were living only by the grace of God. Their continued life was for the purpose of bearing fruit.

It also meant that apparent blessing and abundance were not necessarily something of which one should boast. The tree that had produced no fruit received special

attention and added fertilizer, not because it was so good, but rather because it was so poor.

In order to understand the poignancy of the parable, one has to remember what a vineyard might look like at the time when one would normally come looking for the last possibility of fruit on a fig tree. This would be the early fall. The vineyard would have already yielded its grapes and would have been pruned. It would all have been cut down. One would see nothing but dry and gnarled stumps. In the midst of this scene of apparent desolation, stood a verdant fig tree. It had never been pruned. It had been allowed to grow tall and green. Now, it would receive even further special treatment. The vinedresser would dig around it and give it a special dose of fertilizer.

To a casual observer, the tree would appear to be particularly blessed, and the vines cursed and forgotten. One would think that the fig tree must be especially valuable if it was treated with such care. The truth was exactly the opposite. The fig tree was receiving special care because it had yet to give the fruit it was meant to bear.

In the parable, the owner of the vineyard told the vinedresser to allow the fig tree to continue living, to give it privileged attention, for one more year. This was its last chance. If after that time the tree still had not produced fruit, it would be cut down.

Bear Fruit Worthy of Repentance

This is the point of contact with the stories of the Galileans whom Pilate had murdered and those others on whom the tower fell. Those who were

> But I that wretched tree am, which
> The hunger of my Christ deceives,
> He fruit expects, but I am rich
> In nothing but vain spreading leaves,
> Nor am I wood so fit, and apt
> That of me can a saint be shaped.
>
> Yea, I am that same fig tree vain,
> Which in Christ's vineyard planted was,
> Dressed many years with care, and pain,
> Yet only serve to fill a place:
> I therefore fear the axes wound,
> Because I cumber but the ground.
>
> (From "Contrition," by Ralph Knevet; *Chapters Into Verse*, Vol. 2, edited by R. Atwan and L. Wieder, Oxford University Press, 1993; page 129.)

still alive—those who brought the story to Jesus and those who shook their heads in dismay over these tragedies—were alive by the grace of the owner of the vineyard. They were being given one more chance to bear fruit. Jesus said quite clearly, "Unless you repent, you will all perish just as they did" (5).

The connection of the parable with the theme of repentance immediately brought to mind the preaching of John the Baptist in Luke 3:8: "Bear fruits worthy of repentance." Clearly, in Jesus' parable, the fruit that the fig tree should bear is the repentance to which he referred repeatedly in connection with the two tragedies. By the same token, when he said, "Unless you repent, you will all perish," what he meant was a repentance that bears fruit is a repentance made visible in obedient action.

Dimension 3: What Does the Bible Mean to Us?

A Text to Avoid?

This is a text most of us avoid. It raises a number of thorny questions, particularly the age-old question of why human tragedies occur. When tragedy strikes, the first question we ask is, "Why? Why did my child have to die? What evil had she done? Was it perhaps for some evil I did? Why does famine strike in Africa? Is it perhaps because of some particular sinfulness of the Africans or their leaders? Why did Hurricane Hugo hit the Virgin Islands and not Hispaniola? Why did those people die in the accident at La Guardia airport and not others?" These questions are natural to ask and quite impossible to answer. That is one of the reasons why we tend to stay away from this passage in the Gospel of Luke.

The other reason for avoiding this passage does not answer those questions. Jesus did not give us, as we would have liked, a ready-made answer (like a doctor prescribes a pill to a patient) that we could give to the mother whose teenage son has just died in an automobile accident. Rather, he told us that a certain answer was wrong, and then he moved on to tell us that such tragedies, unexplainable and mysterious though they may be, call survivors to greater obedience.

This passage is particularly poignant to me because I have lost count of the number of times when, speaking to someone about hunger in various parts of the world, I have heard the response that these people are suffering from famine because of their sin. I do agree that famine is the result of human sin, although most likely not the sin of those who are dying. Therefore, upon reading this text, I wonder if Jesus would not

> These words are from Ezekiel 34:18-19. If you read the entire chapter, you will find that often human suffering is the result of human sin, yes, but not necessarily the sin of those who suffer.

have responded with something like, "Do you believe that those Ethiopian children who have starved to death were worse sinners than the rest of Ethiopia, worse sinners than the ruthless and uncaring government under which they lived? Or do you think that those who perished in the earthquake in Los Angeles were worse offenders than all the others?"

When we put the matter in such terms, it is clear that whatever we say about the suffering of those far away must be consistent with what we are ready to say about the tragedies that strike closer to home, or about our own suffering. Otherwise it would be too easy to blame the victims—to say, for instance, that people are poor because they are lazy, or that a certain far-away country is suffering because of its sin.

Whose Sin Results in Suffering?

If we combine this with what the rest of Scripture says, it is clear that at least some suffering is caused by those who appear to be most blessed, or at least strongest. Look, for instance, at what the prophet Ezekiel says. "Is it not enough for you to feed on the good pasture, but you must tread down with your feet the rest of the pasture? When you drink of clear water, must you foul the rest with your feet? And must my sheep eat what you have trodden with your feet, and drink what you have fouled with your feet?"

I, who write this lesson, do not particularly like this parable. I would like to think that the reason why I have a comfortable house, when so many are homeless, and a substantial income, when so many are poor, and all kinds of food to eat, when so many are hungry, and a healthy body, when so many are ill, is that I have somehow been particularly faithful. I would like to think that the reason why I have already lived longer than the average person on this globe is because my life has been so productive.

This text, however, leads me to think otherwise. *Could it be that the reason why I have been given all these advantages is that otherwise I would have great difficulty bearing fruit? Could it be that all these things of which I so pride myself are really just so much manure, piled on me because otherwise I would be such a poor tree?* It is a question I must ponder, a question all who read this text must also ponder.

What is a question for us as individuals is also a question for us as a church and as individual congregations. We tend to admire the big church with the tall steeple, the large staff, and the professional choir. We tend to think that the fact that a church has many resources at its command is a sign that it has been faithful. This parable raises the question that it may really be otherwise. There are some poor churches, both in this country and overseas, churches with no social prestige, churches with no buildings, where one can breathe the Spirit of God, and where one can taste the fruits of mercy and justice. So we must wonder—just wonder—could it be that our own wealth of resources has been given to us in an effort to lead us to bear fruit, to share those resources, to share of ourselves? Could it be that the reason we survive is, not our great budget, our nice music, our fine sermons, our beautiful buildings, our sophisticated theology, but this miraculous grace of the owner of the vineyard who has decided to give us one more chance?

"Those eighteen who were killed when the tower of Siloam fell on them—do you think that they were worse offenders than all the others living in Jerusalem? No, I tell you; but unless you repent, you will all perish just as they did" (4-5).

"If it bears fruit next year, well and good; but if not, you can cut it down" (9).

Dimension 4:
A Daily Bible Journey Plan

Day 1: Luke 15:1-10
Day 2: Luke 15:11-32
Day 3: Luke 16:1-13
Day 4: Luke 16:14-18
Day 5: Luke 16:19-31
Day 6: Luke 17:1-10
Day 7: Luke 17:11-19

10 Lost and Found

Luke 15:1-32

What to Watch For

The fifteenth chapter of Luke consists of three well-known parables of Jesus. Since they are so well known, you will be tempted to read them cursorily, without paying much attention to the text. Don't!

It is often such well-known texts suddenly offer new insight into our Christian life and God's will for us. They do so when we do not take them for granted, but rather study them seriously as if we had never heard them before.

As you read this text, watch for the setting in which Jesus told these parables. He was using them in a particular context to respond to a certain challenge or issue. By placing the parables in that setting, you may gain new insight into their meaning.

Also, look for connecting points among the three parables, or between two of them. When you find several parables together in Luke, they are often trying to make similar points. Thus, the connection among them is important to understand their meaning.

Dimension 1:
What Does the Bible Say?

1. In what setting did Jesus tell these parables? To whom was Jesus speaking? Were they generally friendly or hostile? If hostile, why were they so?

2. Were there any common themes or phrases in all three parables?

3. How did these common themes or phrases respond to the situation in which Jesus was telling the parables?

4. Were there any significant differences or contrasts among the three parables? How did they enrich or complement each other?

Dimension 2:
What Does the Bible Mean?

He Told Them This Parable

Begin by looking at the situation in which Jesus told these parables. You will find the situation given in verses 1 and 2. It is a theme we have encountered before in the Gospel of Luke: the tax collectors and sinners were eager to listen to Jesus, and he welcomed them. In response, the Pharisees and the scribes grumbled and criticized Jesus for the company he kept. Note therefore that when in verse 3 Luke said that "he told them this parable," the "them" to whom Luke referred was not the disciples, but the scribes and Pharisees who had been criticizing him.

The first parable placed these hostile hearers at its very center: "Which one of you . . . ?" In other words, Jesus did not tell this parable, as we often think, to speak of the tremendous love of God, who goes out looking for the lost sheep. He said rather that any person who had a hundred sheep and lost one would look for it. He *expected* that his hearers would do this. Therefore, he expected that they should not be astonished if God did likewise.

In this parable, the owner of the sheep (presumably also their shepherd, although the text does not call him that) was willing to leave the other ninety-nine "in the wilderness." This was not for lack of love. The ninety-nine that were not lost could fend for themselves while the lost one was being sought.

A Lost Sheep

Upon finding this particular sheep, the owner did something that he could not possibly have done for all one hundred sheep: he lay it on his shoulders and rejoiced (5). In other words, this particular sheep, precisely because it was lost, received special attention.

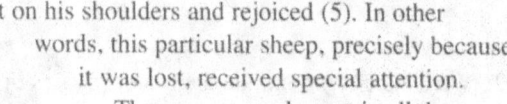

Then comes an element in all these parables that we often miss: the common rejoicing. Not only did the owner of the sheep rejoice, but called "together his friends and neighbors" to celebrate the finding of the sheep (6).

Finally comes the point of the parable: "There will be more joy in heaven over one sinner who repents than over ninety-nine righteous persons who need no repentance" (7). In other words, that is why Jesus was willing to devote so much time and attention to "tax collectors and sinners," even though the Pharisees and the scribes grumbled and even felt left out.

A Lost Coin

The second parable is about a woman. You may remember that in our first lesson we pointed out that Luke was particularly interested in women's participation in God's work. He often paired off parables, one about a man and one about a woman (look, for instance, at the two short parables in Luke 13:18-21), or two miracles (remember the story of the Gerasene demoniac and the woman with hemorrhages). This woman had ten silver coins, or ten drachmas. As in the case of the sheep, one of her coins was lost. At this point, the lost coin became so important that the other nine were not even mentioned again in the parable. The woman centered her attention on the lost coin. She used all the means at her disposal to find the coin (she lighted a lamp, swept, and searched). When she found that one coin, she did something similar to the man with the lost sheep:

she called her friends and neighbors for a celebration. (You may be interested that in Greek there is a masculine and a feminine form of the word for "friends." While the man called his male neighbors, the woman called her female neighbors.)

Then the parable concludes with a point that is similar to the point of the first parable: "There is joy in the presence of the angels of God over one sinner who repents" (10).

A Lost Child

The third parable in this chapter is the one we usually call "the prodigal son"—although there is much more here than a father and a son. Since the parable is so well known, it may be well to point out some elements we might miss.

- The first point is that the one who asked for his portion of the inheritance was the younger son. In the eyes of Jesus' listeners, this would have made his sin even greater. He was the son with the least rights. Yet he insisted on them in a manner that was an affront to his father and even a breach of the commandment to honor your father and your mother.
- Secondly, note that after he had squandered his money, this young man ended up taking care of pigs. For a Jew, this would be the greatest humiliation: taking care of pigs for Gentile masters! Remember, the people who were listening to Jesus were all Jews, and the ones who had criticized him were precisely those Jews who were most stringent about the law. They would immediately understand that the son in this parable had sunk as low as was possible.
- Thirdly, note that the son's repentance did not presume on his relationship to his father. He did not say, "I'll go back and be a cherished son again." He knew that he had forfeited any rights he might have had in his father's house—after all, he had already taken possession of his inheritance and squandered it. He no longer had the rights of an heir.

Then, note that as the son approached, the initiative passed to the father. It was the father who ran, who embraced, who kissed. When the son began to deliver his prepared speech, the father did not let him finish. He took action. He called his slaves and ordered a feast. The son would be dressed in honor, and the fatted calf would be killed so that there would be a great celebration.

And There Was Great Rejoicing

This part of the parable ends, like the other two parables, with a celebration. And the theme of the lost and the found is also sounded here: this son of mine "was dead and has come to life; he was lost and has been found" (32).

To this point, the three parables have been closely parallel to each other. Something that was lost is found, and there is much rejoicing. The owner of the sheep called his friends and neighbors. The woman who found her coin called her (female) friends and neighbors. The father who found his son ordered that the fatted calf be killed for a great celebration.

A New Element

Now, however, a new element is in this third parable: the older son. He was in the field—that is, he was working for his father as a dutiful son. Upon returning, he heard the music and dancing—apparently, this was quite a celebration. When he found out that his brother was back and that the feast was in celebration of his return, rather than join his father in celebration, he became angry and refused to go in.

The dialogue between the elder son and his father is quite illuminating. The elder son called his brother "this son of yours." The father called him "this brother of yours." It soon became clear that the elder son was angry not only at his brother but most especially at his father, who had never even given him "a young goat" and now had killed the fatted calf for this wayward son. In the dialogue, the depth of the elder son's alienation to the father came to light. He felt that he had been working "like a slave"—that is, not like a son. He was begrudging "a young goat," while the father told him that "all that I have is yours."

The parable ends with the father reiterating the reason for the celebration: the dead has come back to life; the lost has been found.

A Strange Place to End

We are left wondering whether the elder son ever came into the house and joined the festivities. It is a strange place to end. But it is the proper place to end, given the setting in which the parable was being told. The parable was being told to Pharisees and scribes who were grumbling because Jesus welcomed tax collectors and sinners. They, the Pharisees and scribes, were like the older son. They had always served and obeyed God. They took extreme care to obey each and every one of God's laws. They had always been around, serving God "like a slave."

Now, Jesus was telling them that tax collectors and sinners (lost sheep, lost coins, lost sons) were coming back to God, and it was time for a great celebration. They were certainly invited, for they, like the elder son, had been faithful servants of God. But if they refused to enter, God would not call off the feast just to please them. Even if they grumbled, the parable would end just as it now does, with the older son standing outside and complaining.

It was for this reason that the parable ends where it does. By leaving the older son still outside, disputing with the father, the end of the story was still undecided. It was up to the older son to decide whether to join the celebration or not. The father would celebrate the return of the prodigal. The older brother should also celebrate the return. But the party would not wait for him. Although he complained to the father, canceling the party was not one of his choices. He could either come in or stay out. If he came in, as a dutiful and loving son and brother, he could share in the fatted calf and in the joy of the family. If he was angry enough to stay out, the tables would be turned. He who had always served his father faithfully would be the one alienated, just as much as if he had gone to a distant land and squandered his father's inheritance.

> Do you think that the scribes and the Pharisees got the point?

Dimension 3:
What Does the Bible Mean to Us?

We can apply these parables to our lives in different ways according to where we place ourselves in them. (It is quite possible that at different stages in our lives, or even at different moments, we may find ourselves at different places in the parables.)

In the first place, and most importantly, we may see ourselves as the lost who have been found. We can see ourselves playing this role for two different reasons.

The first of these—and one of which we normally might not think—is that most of us are Gentiles. Most of us do not belong to the original people of God. We are not children of Abraham and Sarah according to the flesh. Yet, by the grace of God, we have been made heirs of the promises made to Abraham and Sarah. We who were "no people" have been made a people.

But secondly, and touching each of us more directly, we each were lost in our own sin and **would not have been found except for the amaz-**

ing grace of God. We are the lost sheep, the lost coin, the prodigal son for which heaven rejoices. And we rejoice with heaven that there is a feast laid out for us—wayward children that we are. It is true that some of us may not remember a time when we were completely lacking in faith, literally "in a distant land." But even in that case, we know that, were it not for the grace of God, we would be nothing but lost sinners.

This way of reading the parables, however, does not suffice. We must keep coming back to them constantly in order to remember that we are the lost whom Jesus has saved. But we must also read the parables as a warning.

The parables are a warning because, in a way, we are much closer to the Pharisees and the scribes than to the publicans and sinners. The Pharisees and scribes were the religious people of their time. No one took as much care as a Pharisee to find out what the law meant in every circumstance of life and to apply and obey it to the letter. No one took as much care as the scribes to read Scripture, to memorize it, to make certain that not a word of it was lost or forgotten. Indeed, the scribes even knew how many letters there were in each book of the Bible. Thus, by counting the letters, they could make certain that not one had been omitted or added.

In coming together for Bible study and trying to know as much as possible about the Bible, we are very much like the scribes. In trying to find out, as we do in this section, what the Bible means to us, we are very much like the Pharisees. We cannot avoid it. That is who we are: generally good, religious people who try to serve God.

For this reason, the temptations of the Pharisee and the scribe are also ours. Jesus did not attack the scribes for their knowledge of Scripture. Jesus did not attack the Pharisees for their attempts to be as obedient as possible. Jesus criticized them because they thought that they, and they alone, had an "inside track" with God. In consequence, they despised the tax collectors and the "sinners," and could not bear Jesus welcoming them.

We cannot help it. That is who we are. We may have been the younger son, the prodigal who returned to God's embrace. But right now we are also the older son, the faithful one, the one who has been serving the father all along. And we too are tempted to begrudge the father's liberality toward the younger one who has gone astray and is now ready to return.

Have we ever seen or experienced the kind of religiosity that, while apparently faithful to God, is in fact alienated from God? Remember the son who

> The story of the two sons does not end. Jesus left the older son outside the father's house, disputing with the father, precisely in order to leave the option open. He was not saying that there is no place for the Pharisee and the scribe. He was saying that the Pharisee and the scribe, just like the tax collector and the sinner, have to come into the feast on God's terms, not theirs.

said he had worked for his father "like a slave." Is there a type of religion that, serving God faithfully but "as a slave," loses the joy of it? Are we ever tempted by that kind of religiosity?

Called to Be Imitators

Finally, we may read these parables as a call to be imitators of the God who seeks the lost and welcomes them when they are found. If we really believe that we are like that lost sheep, that lost coin, or that lost son, and that we have been found and brought in by the grace of God, then we shall make every possible effort to continue God's work of searching for the lost.

We may be like the younger son who went to a distant country and had a long way to return. Or we may be like the older son who never left and for that very reason risked being alienated from his father. Most probably, we are like both. But no matter what, God is inviting us to the great feast of celebration for the return of all that was lost. (Remember, all three parables end with celebrations.)

Having accepted the invitation to the feast, having been found, we have no option but to be imitators of the shepherd who looks for the hundredth sheep, the woman who looks for the tenth coin, and the father who welcomes the second son.

Is the faith we live, and the manner in which we express it, such as to invite others to come into the feast? Is our congregational life such that we are really imitators of and witness to the God who calls in tax collectors and sinners?

JESUS' PARABLES ACCORDING TO LUKE

The Sower—Luke 8:5-8
The Good Samaritan—Luke 10:30-35
The Rich Fool—Luke 12:16-20
The Fig Tree—Luke 13:6-9
The Mustard Seed—Luke 13:18-19
Leaven—Luke 13:20-21
The Great Supper—Luke 14:16-24
The Tower Builder—Luke 14:28-30
The Warring King—Luke 14:31-32
The Lost Sheep—Luke 15:4-6
The Lost Coin—Luke 15:8-9
The Prodigal Son (the Lost Son)—Luke 15:11-32
The Unjust Steward—Luke 16:1-8a
The Rich Man and Lazarus—Luke 16:9-31
The Unjust Judge—Luke 18:2-5
The Pharisee and the Tax Collector—Luke 18:10-13
The Talents—Luke 19:11-27
The Evil Tenants—Luke 20:9-18

Dimension 4:
A Daily Bible Journey Plan

Day 1: **Luke 17:20-37**
Day 2: **Luke 18:1-17**
Day 3: **Luke 18:18-30**
Day 4: **Luke 18:31-34**
Day 5: **Luke 18:35-43**
Day 6: **Luke 19:1-10**
Day 7: **Luke 19:11-27**

11 Learning From a Scoundrel

Luke 16:1-15

What to Watch For

The study of this parable is instructive at several levels:

- There is the teaching of the parable itself, which we will try to elucidate.

- This parable helps us to understand how Jesus used parables. We often think that parables are moral examples, little vignettes of life to be imitated in all things. In this parable the main character is a scoundrel. Still, Jesus used him as an example. What are we to make of that?

- As you read this text, try to see the point that Jesus made with the parable. Do not allow your sense of outrage at the dishonest steward to hide the meaning of the parable from you. Jesus told this parable in order to convey a message. What is that message?

INTRODUCING A PARABLE

A parable is a short story with a double meaning. On one level the parable discusses ordinary life events such as farming, sheep raising, or harvesting. On a deeper level the parables of Jesus caused listeners to reflect on the Kingdom.

INTRODUCING A STEWARD

Several different terms used in the Bible are translated as "steward." In general, a *steward* is a person who takes care of something or oversees something on behalf of someone else. In the New Revised Standard Version translation of Luke 16:1-9, the word is translated as "manager." In our time, someone might hire a manager to "manage" one's business or career affairs. In biblical times, a managing steward may have been a hireling or a slave entrusted with important oversight tasks within a wealthy person's household.

Dimension 1: What Does the Bible Say?

1. Last week we heard Jesus addressing the crowds. With whom did Jesus share this parable?

2. Why do you think that we seldom hear sermons on this parable? Does it have nothing to tell us? What do you think its message is?

3. How did the Pharisees react when they apparently overheard what Jesus was telling his disciples? What was Jesus' response?

Dimension 2: What Does the Bible Mean?

A Parable About a Squanderer

Last week we studied three parables that Jesus told the crowds in response to the grumblings of the Pharisees and scribes. This week, we study a parable that, according to Luke, Jesus told to his disciples, but the Pharisees somehow overheard.

The parable begins by speaking of a rich man; in truth the main character of the parable is the rich man's steward. The rich man learned that the steward had been "squandering his property" (Luke 16:1). This phrase (the same one used in Luke 15:13 about the prodigal) did not necessarily mean that the steward was guilty of pocketing his master's money. It meant simply that he was not a good manager. He could have been taking his master's money, or he could simply have been managing it unwisely. We do not know. In any case the specifics behind the phrase "squandered his property" do not affect the point of the parable.

> Stewards often were slaves who had been raised to that position while still remaining slaves; in this case the rest of the story implies that the steward was a free man who, once fired, would have to fend for himself.

Having received such news, the rich man called the manager and asked for a final account, telling him that his position as steward would be taken from him.

The steward now found himself in a difficult position. He had been given notice, and he had a short time in which to think about the future. He had to think of a way to make a living. This was not easy, for he could not do physical work. Once his firing took effect, all he would be able to do is beg—and he would be ashamed to do that. The realism of the parable is remarkable. Those who first heard it must have known many a steward like this one. The steward, accustomed as he was to light work and to the prestige of managing his master's riches, was either too old or too out of shape to do physical labor; he was too proud to beg after having been a person of such importance.

He therefore came up with a third alternative. Rather than preparing to work or to beg, he took steps so that "people may welcome [him] into their homes" (4). In order to understand this, we have to remember that in that culture the laws of hospitality and of mutuality required that favors received be returned. On the basis of these principles, this steward decided that he would turn his master's debtors into his own friends—or at least his debtors. *So he cheated*—there is no other word for it. The parable tells us that he called in two of these debtors and told them to fix their bills. The man who owed the master a hundred jugs of olive oil would only repay fifty, and the one who owed a hundred containers of wheat would repay eighty. Although the parable does not say so, it is implied that what he did with these two creditors he also did with a number of others, in order to have his future assured.

The Surprise of the Parable

We would expect Jesus to say that this was an evil example that we should all avoid. Surprise! That was not what he said. The dishonest steward was commended for his shrewdness! (Who actually commended him poses a problem for interpreters. The words that the NRSV translates as "his master" (8) are really "the master." Therefore, it is not clear if Jesus said that the master in the parable commended the steward, or if Luke said that Jesus, "the master," commended the steward. In any case, this makes little difference for the meaning of the parable. The important point is that the steward was commended for his dishonest behavior.)

The reason why the master commended the dishonest steward was that he had acted cleverly. The word used implies the kind of shrewdness that would be good in business. Thus this steward, although not a very good manager of his master's riches, proved that when it really mattered he had a good business sense.

The reason why the steward acted in this manner was that "the children of this age are more shrewd in dealing with their own generation than are the children of light" (8). The "children of this age" (or eon, or world) knew how to deal with the realities of life and to make the best of them in their own limited context, as did this dishonest steward. Meanwhile, the "children of light," who obviously had to live also in "this generation," but who were not part of "this age," were not as shrewd. They did not know how to make use of the goods that had been temporarily entrusted to them as cleverly as did this scoundrel of a steward.

The application or explanation of the parable continues in verses 9-13. The point is that Jesus' disciples were to make friends for themselves by means of "dishonest wealth" (9) so that they could be welcomed in the eternal homes (or, more literally, "tents"). The phrase "dishonest wealth," or "unrighteous mammon," may cause some difficulties. Scholars are not in full agreement as to their exact meaning. What is clear is that Jesus was referring to the goods of this life. Apparently, he called them "unrighteous" because they belonged to the present, unrighteous order. Note that in verse 11 the phrase appears again, this time in contrast with "the true riches." Whatever else it might mean, the "dishonest wealth" clearly referred to the goods of the present life, while the "true riches" referred to life "in the eternal homes."

> The immediate and most important teaching of the parable is that the disciples, like shrewd stewards, were to use whatever means they now had—even if this was an unrighteous order—to prepare for the time when they would wish to be welcome in the heavenly homes.

Commended for Shrewdness

The dishonest steward was commended for his shrewdness in dealing with his master's wealth once he knew he was about to be fired. A man in his position had too few other options. On the one hand, he could say to himself: "These riches will no longer be mine. Therefore, I better forget about them and think about something else. From now on, I will have nothing to do with my master's affairs." On the other hand, he could have said: "Since I know that I am about to be fired, I might as well enjoy these riches while I have access to them. It may be a short time that I have, but I might as well make the best of it." This steward chose neither of those things. On the contrary, he said to himself: "I am being fired. A new order is coming in which I will no longer have control over these things. The wisest thing to do is to use the time that I have and the control over these things that I still have to prepare for the new order." In this situation he showed remarkable shrewdness, and "the master" (whoever that might be) commended him for it.

The further explanation of the parable includes verses 10-13—a complicated series of sayings that we will analyze in the class session. The point is clear. The steward was shrewd because he knew how to use the passing riches of his master for his future safety and well-being. So should the disciples of Jesus be equally shrewd and use the wealth and other resources of the present life and the present order in light of the future that is coming. Note that "wealth" or "mammon," which is depicted in verse 12 as a means to attain the "true riches," is characterized in verse 13 as an an idol that competes with God. Thus, it is clear that Jesus was saying that, while serving the goods of this world is a form of idolatry, and disciples must certainly avoid that, those goods themselves can be used in such a way that one is entrusted with the "true riches"—or, that one is welcome in the eternal homes. This was what the steward did, why the master commended him, and the sense in which he was an example for the disciples.

The Pharisees Were Astonished

Meanwhile the Pharisees, who apparently had been standing by, heard what Jesus was teaching and began mocking him. Luke implied that they ridiculed Jesus because they were "lovers of money." Apparently they did not like the radical opposition that Jesus established between serving God and serving riches, so that one could not do both. Or perhaps they reacted to the parable the same way many of us do, in astonishment that Jesus could take such a scoundrel for an example.

In any case, Jesus now turned and spoke directly to them. His words were harsh. The Pharisees, he said, justified themselves before others. That, however, was to no avail, for God knew what was in their hearts. What was in their hearts was the prizing of wealth, prestige, and self-justification in such a way that it was an abomination before God. In other words, they were prime examples of what Jesus had been talking about, the desire to serve both God and mammon, to be fully committed both to God's will on the one hand and to having prestige and power in the present order on the other, as if it were possible to serve two masters.

Dimension 3: What Does the Bible Mean to Us?

A Troubling Role Model

What makes this text difficult is that Jesus took a thief, a rascal, and used him as an example for us. The parable of a sower spoke of a man who worked for a living. The woman who put the leaven in the dough was also working. The parable about the talents spoke of three stewards who tried to do their best. All of those persons were characters worthy of imitation, and their stories are often told in Christian preaching and in Christian art. Can you imagine a stained-glass window where a character with a shifty look tells another, "Where it says a hundred, put down eighty"?

Yet, in spite of all this, as we reflect on this parable, we realize that it makes much sense, for it accurately describes our situation.

- The steward seemed quite settled in his position when he received the fateful news. His stewardship would be taken from him. What he would have liked to be permanent will not be so. We are in a similar condition. Sometimes we are so settled into life, managing and enjoying its goods, that we convince ourselves that we have a permanent post here. We forget that the human condition is such that when we least expect it, we may be fired. Thus, perhaps like the steward in the parable, we go about our business administering the things of life and enjoying its goods, as if our tenure would never end.
- There is more. Like the steward in the parable, we have all been fired—at least, we have been given notice. The parable does not tell us how many days' notice the steward received. Nor do we know how many days are left until our firing is effective. *The fact remains that we are all on notice!*

In the previous section, we saw that the steward had at least two other options he could have followed. On one extreme, he simply could have refused to have anything more to do with his master's wealth. On the other extreme, he could have decided that, since he had been fired, he would "live it up" with that wealth, as long as he still had use of it.

Put on Notice

We too have the same options as the steward. We know that we have been fired, that the present order is passing. What then shall we do with our present tenure? One possible answer follows this line of thinking: "I will enjoy all I can. Life is short, and I am going to enjoy it." That is a common answer in our day when people are frantically trying to make more money, to have more experiences, to enjoy more things. The second answer is also common among Christians: "Since all this order is passing, I shall ignore and forget it. The material things of this life can lead me away from God. Therefore, I shall ignore them, and pretend that they do not exist."

None of these, however, is the shrewd answer commended in the parable. The shrewd answer is to acknowledge that our tenure with these goods is limited and then to see how we can use them, not in view of the present order, but in view of the future.

This parable builds on a theme that we have encountered repeatedly in our study of Luke: the expectation of the kingdom or reign of God as the basis for the disciples' life and actions. It is a parable of stewardship, not just because it mentions a steward, but because its intention is to guide us in the administration of the goods we have received—goods that include life, health, time, talents, money, and so forth.

We live in a world where the worship of "mammon" is rampant. All around us, we see people whose main goal in life is to amass wealth and possessions. As part of this society, as people of our own generation (8), we are tempted to live by the same principles.

Often we succumb to that temptation. In one way or another, we all do. In the space below, make an inventory of the last week of your life. *Have you succumbed to the temptation to amass wealth?*

```
┌─────────────────────────────────────────────┐
│           A PERSONAL INVENTORY              │
│                                             │
│                                             │
│                                             │
│                                             │
│                                             │
│                                             │
└─────────────────────────────────────────────┘
```

Fired From the Present Order

The goods of this world do matter. We are living in a world in which people die for lack of some of those goods. As we saw in another lesson, such people and their physical sufferings do matter to Jesus and should matter also to Christians. To think that we can go through this life without paying attention to material goods and their administration is as un-Christian as to think that we can devote this life to the worship of mammon.

What we must do, like that dishonest but shrewd steward, is to make an inventory of the goods we now have—and will certainly not have forever—and see how we can use them in the service of the coming reign of God. Like the steward, we have been fired from the present order. We are on notice. But we also have the promise of a new order—in our case, the reign of God. Can we learn to manage our affairs as people who really believe in that future order? We had better, since we have all been given notice of firing from the present order!

As you conclude your study of this lesson, make an inventory of the "goods" you have in the present order. Think not only of money but also of time, abilities, relationships, and position.

AN INVENTORY OF MY GOODS

Ask yourself, *How can I begin to manage these goods as a steward who knows he or she has been fired, but is looking forward to the new order?* Finally, give some consideration to the same question, but now in terms of your entire study group. *What goods do we have that as stewards we would be managing differently if we were really doing it in light of the coming reign of God?*

Dimension 4:
A Daily Bible Journey Plan

Day 1: Luke 19:28-40
Day 2: Luke 19:41-48
Day 3: Luke 20:1-19
Day 4: Luke 20:20-26
Day 5: Luke 20:27-47
Day 6: Luke 21:1-19
Day 7: Luke 21:20-38

12 — The Crucifixion
Luke 23:26-49

What to Watch For

We come to the last two lessons of our study, but the most important. Everything in Luke's Gospel has been leading to these two momentous events: the death and resurrection of Jesus. As the drama unfolds, we come to the realization that it is toward the cross that Jesus has been moving ever since his birth.

As we come to this point, we realize that, at both a human and political level, the way to the cross was paved by a series of encounters with the religious and political leaders of Israel. Tension has been mounting, and finally these forces take their revenge.

At a deeper level, Luke has also shown us that there is a greater will leading Jesus to the cross. Oddly enough, it is a will of love. Jesus knew it and repeatedly told his disciples; they did not understand. No matter. Eventually they would.

As you approach these two lessons, the two great mysteries of our redemption, take time to pray. Take time to bow before the mystery of God's awesome love. Take time to let God speak to your inner soul, friend to friend, mystery to mystery. Listen... pray... be silent.... God speaks....

Dimension 1:
What Does the Bible Say?

1. Try to read the text as if you had never heard it before. Who are the various witnesses and participants in the Crucifixion? What do they do?

2. As you read this story, quite apart from all the other narratives of the Crucifixion in the other Gospels, what strikes you? Is this consistent with what we have learned about Luke and his Gospel throughout these lessons?

Dimension 2:
What Does the Bible Mean?

A Miscarriage of Justice

The text begins after the trial of Jesus. Luke has made it clear that the trial was a miscarriage of justice. Pilate declared Jesus innocent three times (23:4, 13-14, 22). Eventually, however, at the insistence of "the chief priests, the leaders, and the people" (23:13), he handed Jesus over to be crucified.

Now Jesus was on the way to the place of execution, and a certain Simon of Cyrene was forced to carry the cross behind Jesus. Luke told us no more about this Simon, although many stories, legends, and conjectures have been woven around him.

As Jesus and Simon were walking toward the place of Crucifixion, "a great number of the people followed him, and among them were women." Here Luke brought to the foreground two themes that are characteristic both of his Gospel and of Acts. The first is "the people." Throughout his two books, Luke made it clear that "the people" often were receptive, first to Jesus, and later to his disciples, and that it was their leaders who led them astray. In the trial, the leading role in the prosecution belonged to "the assembly of the elders of the people, both chief priests and scribes" (22:66). Later, before Pilate, it was "the chief priests, the leaders, and the people" who finally came together to demand that Jesus be crucified. Now on the way to the cross, "a great number of the people followed him."

From the context, and from Luke's choice of words, it was clear that they followed, not to mock or as spectators, but because they were moved by what was taking place.

Among these people, Luke singled out some "women who were beating their breasts and wailing" (23:27). These actions were signs of sorrow. To these women Jesus turned and uttered a crushing prophecy: "Do not weep for me, but weep for yourselves and your children" (28). He declared that the coming times would be so terrible that having children, traditionally a blessing in ancient culture, would be considered a curse, and people would cry to have the mountains crush them.

His analysis of the situation was deeply perceptive of what history tells us eventually happened: "For if they do this when the wood is green, what will happen when it is dry?" (31) In other words, these events took place when things were not ready for a conflagration. The interest of the leaders of the people in preserving their power and prestige, and the weakness of Roman authorities, brought this event about even at a time of relative peace. They had managed to light this fire of injustice, even though the wood was green. But as time passed, the wood would become dry. The injustice and the mismanagement that led Jesus to the cross would increase. Eventually, the resultant fire would be all consuming.

They Crucified Him

We now learn that Jesus was not to be crucified alone. There were two others to be killed with him. Luke did not tell us why they were being crucified. He simply said that they were criminals. The place assigned for Crucifixion was called "The Skull," apparently because of the shape of the hill. (Luke translated the word *Golgotha*, which the other evangelists left in the original Hebrew and Aramaic. The name *Calvary* came from the Latin for "skull," *calvarium*.)

> Hear, Shepherd! thou who for thy flock art dying.
> O wash away these scarlet sins, for thou
> Rejoicest at the contrite sinner's vow.
> O, wait!—the thee my weary soul is crying—
> Wait for me!—Yet why ask it, when I see,
> With feet nailed to the cross, thou art waiting still for me.
>
> ———
> From "The Good Shepherd," by Félix Lope de Vega Carpio (translated by Henry Wadsworth Longfellow)

Luke was shockingly brief. At the crucial point in his story, he simply said "they crucified Jesus" (33). He did not describe the act of crucifixion. Theophilus and Luke's other readers would probably have witnessed other crucifixions. In any case, the horror of what is taking place is made starker by the bluntness of these words: "They crucified Jesus."

And Many Watched

As you read the text, notice that Luke contrasts "the people" and their supposed leaders. "The people stood by, watching, but the leaders scoffed at him" (35). Another crucial element is brought into the story: the presence and acquiescence of the Roman Empire. "The soldiers also mocked him" (36). The sign that hung over him in an attempt at cruel irony reminds us of both powers, the Empire and the Jewish religious establishment: "This is the King of the Jews" (38).

Then follows the scene between the two thieves and Jesus. For a space of five verses (39-43), Luke ignored all else around the tragic scene and for a moment makes us feel as if there was no one there but these three men, with their common suffering. One of the thieves, in his torment, still mocked Jesus. The other intervened, rebuked him, and then turned to Jesus. "Jesus, remember me when you come into your kingdom" (42). What could this man know about the kingdom of Jesus? Probably very little, except that was what the sign said. He may have heard something about this preacher who had recently arrived in Jerusalem. Yet somehow he believed that Jesus, who now hung on a cross with a sign over his head, would someday become a king, as the sign said. So, looking at that distant future, he said: "Jesus, remember me when you come into your kingdom." Jesus, who had not said a word to his tormentors, replied with a promise, not for some distant future, but for now. "Truly I tell you, today you will be with me in Paradise."

According to Luke 22:66, the trial of Jesus before the assembly began "when day came." Then followed the process that took Jesus before Pilate, then before Herod, and finally back to Pilate. Events moved swiftly. It was still the same day, at noon, and Jesus was already hanging on the cross.

Hours of Quiet Torment

Follow the three hours of quiet torment. Once again Luke showed his inimitable feeling for the dramatic in that he said not a word of what Jesus or other people did or said. He turned his attention elsewhere, and said that "darkness came over the whole land until three in the afternoon, while the sun's light failed; and the curtain of the temple was torn in two" (44-45). There has been much discussion about the meaning of the reference to the curtain of the Temple. Perhaps later, during the class session, you will have an opportunity to discuss this reference. For the present, simply note that Luke was conveying the fact that the Crucifixion was not simply an injustice, or a tragedy, or even a sad example of human cruelty. The Crucifixion had an impact on the created world (the sun darkened) as well as the religious world (the curtain of the Temple was rent).

Finally, after commending himself to God in a loud cry, Jesus breathed his last.

To close the scene, Luke reviewed the attitudes of some of the persons around the cross. The Roman centurion saw the injustice of what had been done. "Certainly this man was innocent" (47). Here, Luke prepared the way for his next volume, where some Gentiles will prove to be open to the gospel, and where Roman officials will often take relatively noncommittal stances. The crowds returned home "beating their breasts" (48). In spite of all that the leaders of the people have said and done, Jesus was still a source of hope for the crowds. At a distance stood "the women who had followed him from Galilee" (49). These were the same women who provided financial support for Jesus and his disciples (Luke 8:1-3).

> Note that Luke began his story of the Crucifixion with a reference to the women of Jerusalem and ended his story with a reference to the women from Galilee.

With the women stood also "all his acquaintances" (49) — a word Luke seldom used. Do they include those whom Luke calls the "disciples"? We do not know, although probably not. At any rate, even the women from Galilee and these other acquaintances watch from afar. At the cross, Jesus was alone. There was a crowd watching; there were soldiers guarding and supervising; there were leaders of the people mocking; there were criminals arguing and pleading; but he was alone — alone with the sins of the world!

> Oh! Good, Good, Good, my Lord. What more Love yet.
> Thou dy for mee! What, am I dead in thee?
> What did Deaths arrow shot at me thee hit?
> Didst slip between that flying shaft and mee?
> Didst make thyselfe Deaths marke shot at for mee?
> So that her Shaft shall fly no far than thee?
>
> ---
>
> From "Meditation One Hundred and Twelve," by Edward Taylor, from *The Poetical Works of Edward Taylor*, ed. by Thomas H. Johnson (Princeton Paperback, 1966); copyright Rockland, 1939; Princeton University Press, 1943.

Dimension 3: What Does the Bible Mean to Us?

There is so much to say, and so little that can be said! The significance of this passage is so vast that all our words and all our thoughts fall far short of it. Thus, our first response before the mystery of the Crucifixion must be one of awed silence. We do not know—we can never know in this life—all that it means. Yet, we know that it means all to us.

In Between Christmas and the Crucifixion

The Crucifixion brought to completion what was begun at Christmas. When Jesus was born, he lay in a manger among animals. When he died, he was hanging from a cross between criminals. For us he lay in the manger, and for us he hung from the cross. He whose earthly life began by being treated like an animal, ended that life by being treated like a criminal. And all that for us!

At the beginning of the story a Galilean woman received the unexpected news of his birth. At the end, Galilean women watched in sorrow from a distance. At the beginning of the story, the glory of the Lord shone upon shepherds in the middle of the night. At the end, the very light of the sun failed at noon. And in between—between manger and cross—he healed the sick; he fed the masses; he taught any who would listen; he chastised those who would not.

We know that this is not really the end of the story. We know that he rose again, and that he still heals the sick, feeds the masses, teaches any who will listen, and chastises those who will not. We know that the cross does not have the final word.

Let us take care not to move too hastily from cross to Resurrection. The cross was real. **The cross is real!** The Resurrection certainly overcomes it, but does not take it away!

Let us therefore linger for a while at the cross and see what might be its significance for us. Furthermore, let us look quite simply at Luke's telling of it, for each evangelist had his own perspective on the story, and each helps us see the message from a different angle.

Three Levels of Response

As we read that story, we find three levels of response to Jesus and therefore of relationship with him. We find first of all those who mocked him. Significantly, in this response there was agreement between the leaders of the people, the Roman soldiers who stood by the cross, and one of the criminals who was also being crucified. The leaders scoffed, the soldiers mocked, and the criminal derided. Secondly, there were the women from

Galilee and the acquaintances of Jesus. They stood and watched from afar. Finally, there was the criminal who asked that Jesus remember him. Of all three, it was only this criminal who was really in touch with Jesus.

- The first group, the mockers, included people who were or had been powerful and important. The leaders of the people included the religious and social elite of Israel. The soldiers represented the great Roman Empire. The criminal was used to having his way and was still insisting on it while hanging from the cross. Most likely we are not like this group. We do not mock Jesus. We respect and love him—or do we really? When we fail to take his teachings seriously, do we not mock him? When we flaunt our power and prestige, as if they really mean something, do we not mock him? When we insist on having our own way, do we not mock him? Above all, it is important and painful to remember that the leaders of the people scoffed at Jesus precisely because they were religious—just as we are. They "knew" that God would act precisely as they expected, and they could accept no other action from God. So they scoffed.

> Are we so sure of our own religion, so much "in control" of God, that we will scoff at any divine action we do not understand?

- More than likely, however, we are like the women and the acquaintances, standing at a distance and watching. Like the women who followed Jesus all the way from Galilee, we too wish to follow him. We actually do follow him most of the time. Like them, we are even willing to support his work with our financial resources. When things get difficult, however, when obedience requires risk, we stand aside and watch from a distance.
- Finally, there was the penitent criminal. He began by recognizing that he was guilty and that he had reason to be in the situation in which he found himself. He made no excuses. He did not even make promises. He simply commended himself to Jesus. And he was rewarded by a magnificent promise!

Hard Choices to Be Made

Before the cross of Jesus, there are some hard choices to be made. The leaders of the people, although they served a God who had repeatedly surprised them, were unwilling to be surprised. The soldiers and the one criminal refused to acknowledge a power over them. The women and the acquaintances stood at a distance. One man, a convicted criminal about to die, found life as he hung from his own cross! The difference? The criminal had nothing to lose, no hope to save himself, no social standing to protect. He could be open to Jesus, and Jesus could enter into his open life.

What about us? Are we claiming that Jesus is our Savior and still trying to save ourselves through our prestige, through our financial security, through our social standing, perhaps even through our religious practices? Are we ready to come before our Savior with no pretense of being able to save ourselves? Are we ready to come before our Savior by simply surrendering our all to him? That is part of what he meant by taking up our cross. He said it quite clearly. If we really wish to be his disciples, there is no other way than the way of the cross!

Dimension 4:
A Daily Bible Journey Plan

Day 1: Luke 22:1-13
Day 2: Luke 22:14-30
Day 3: Luke 22:31-38
Day 4: Luke 22:39-53
Day 5: Luke 22:54-71
Day 6: Luke 23:1-12
Day 7: Luke 23:13-25

13

Luke 24:13-35

The Walk to Emmaus

What to Watch For

This is our last study on the Gospel of Luke. As you read the biblical text for this lesson, try to focus both on the story itself and on the details that connect this particular story with some of the themes we have seen elsewhere in the Gospel of Luke.

Perhaps the best way to do this is to read the story at least three times.

- Read it first all at once, trying to get the general sweep of the narrative. This is a resurrection story, and the Resurrection is the high point of the Gospel. Do not miss that point by centering prematurely on all the details of the story.

- Read the text again, this time more slowly, looking at some of the details that make Luke's narrative so interesting and engaging. Note the changing moods of the disciples, and how those moods are expressed both in their words and in their gestures and actions (how and when they stop, what they discuss, or how they comment on the story of Jesus).

- Finally, read the story a third time, now looking for answers to the questions in Dimension 1.

Dimension 1: What Does the Bible Say?

As you read the text, ask how this story picks up on some of the common themes and characteristics we have seen in the rest of the Gospel of Luke:

1. Jesus as the one who did wonders (Remember the miracles we have studied?)

2. Jesus as teacher.

3. Luke's interest in women as active participants in the gospel story.

4. Luke's interest in the meals that Jesus attended.

Dimension 2: What Does the Bible Mean?

On the First Day of the Week

The events that Luke narrated in this passage took place "on that same day" (13). This would be on "the first day of the week" (1), in which several women went to the tomb and received the wonderful news that Jesus had risen. It was also the same day that Peter, having heard the news from the women, ran to the tomb and found it empty.

Now, on that same day, two of the followers of Jesus were going to the nearby village of Emmaus. The text does not say why they were going to Emmaus, and therefore the common comment that they were going because they thought the story of Jesus had ended has no foundation in the text itself. Quite possibly, since Emmaus was relatively close to Jerusalem, they were going there because that is where they lived, with no thought that this meant leaving behind the community of disciples in Jerusalem.

Later on, the text tells us that they were walking. As they walked, they

> We usually think that there were three women who visited the tomb on that first Easter, because three are mentioned by name; but Luke tells us that there were "other women with them" (10).

talked. The word that Luke uses in verse 15 has the connotation of "questioning" or "inquiring." In other words, they were puzzled as they talked about the events in Jerusalem.

As we think of this story, we often imagine that these two disciples had no idea that Jesus had risen. That was not the case. They had heard the report of the women and of others who had also gone to the tomb. Therefore, they were not simply dejected because Jesus had been crucified. They were probably dejected but also hoping against hope that the reports they had heard might be true. Their puzzled conversation revolved precisely around those two points: what to make of Jesus' crucifixion and what to make of the reports of the women and of the others who had found the tomb to be empty.

As they walked and talked, Jesus joined them. At a time when most people traveled on foot, it was customary for strangers to walk together. This provided both relief from the boredom of long walks and relative safety against possible attacks by bandits (remember the parable of the good Samaritan, where a man traveling from Jerusalem to Jericho was attacked by bandits). Therefore, there was nothing odd about a stranger joining these two travelers and entering into their conversation.

The Disciples Do Not Recognize Jesus

Jesus, however, came incognito. Luke tells us that "their eyes were kept from recognizing him" (16). Whether this was because the resurrected Jesus did not necessarily look like the one they had known, or for some other reason, Luke did not tell us. The implication of the entire story is that the real reason why they did not recognize him was that Jesus did not want them to do so.

Jesus questioned them about the subject of their conversation. Apparently even after he joined them, they continued discussing the same subject. They were surprised that he did not know what they were talking about.

Luke adroitly depicted their surprise by saying that "they stood still" (17). Even today this is a fairly common occurrence. We are walking along with someone, and suddenly something they say makes us stop. It is almost as if the surprise will not allow us to continue walking and talking at the same time. We must stop and concentrate on whatever has surprised us.

This was what these disciples did. They stopped and stood still. They were sad. Luke does not tell us if they were sad because Jesus had been crucified, or sad because this stranger showed that what to them was so important could be completely unknown to others.

Finally, one of them expressed their surprise. "Are you the only stranger in Jerusalem who does not know the things that have taken place there in these days?" (18) The word the the NRSV translates as "stranger" (18) actually means "sojourner." The emphasis is not so much on being alien as on being a temporary resident. Obviously, since Jesus had joined them on the road, and they were practically on the outskirts of Jerusalem and walking away from the city, they assumed that he too was coming from Jerusalem, and that he was now continuing on a journey after a stop in Jerusalem.

The Disciples Retell the Story

Jesus asked them about the news they were discussing, and they told him. Since it was not customary in ancient writings to record conversations verbatim, one may surmise that Luke did not wish us to think that the words we read are exactly what they said. Presumably, since they had a relatively long walk, they would have given many more details than Luke quoted here. In any case, their words were a summary of the early preaching of the church, although obviously they were still hesitant on the crucial point of the Resurrection, which would eventually become central to that preaching. What they told him was first of all that Jesus of Nazareth was "a prophet mighty in deed and word" (19). This idea summarizes much of what we have read in weeks past about Jesus' miracles (deed) and teachings (word).

> Luke informs us that this particular disciple's name was Cleopas. Luke did this at other points in his narrative. Remember, for instance, that it was in the middle of the story that he told us that the Pharisee in whose house Jesus was eating was called Simeon.

This prophet was "handed over" (20) (presumably to the Roman authorities) by "our chief priest and leaders." Here we see the familiar Lukan theme: that it was the leaders of the people who opposed both Jesus and the early church. In contrast, says Cleopas, "We had hoped that he was the one to redeem Israel" (21).

This circumstance, however, was not the entire cause of their puzzlement. That by itself would have led to disappointment and dejection. There is now added a puzzling note: "Some women of our group astounded us" (22). In brief words, Cleopas retold the story of the women at the tomb, and then added that "some of those who were with us" (24)—not just Peter, as in Luke 24:12—went and found the tomb empty, "but they did not see him" (24). In other words, there were several indications of the Resurrection, but they did not know for a fact that it was true, nor did they know what to make of it in any case.

Apparently, although he still did not make himself known to them, Jesus did keep his aura of authority, for he responded by calling them "foolish" and "slow of heart" (25) and still they listened to his exposition of the Scriptures. The gist of that exposition is that it was "necessary that the Messiah should suffer" (26). In other words, the cross, far from being a denial of Jesus' messiahship, is its confirmation.

The Disciples' Eyes Were Opened

Eventually they reached the village of Emmaus and, as was normal in the hospitality code of the time, Jesus did not presume that they would invite him to stay with them; but they did.

Then came the climactic point of the entire story. It took place "when he was at the table with them" (30). (Remember how many other times throughout Luke's Gospel that Jesus was at table with his disciples, or with "publicans and sinners," or with Pharisees.) The last time that Luke told us that Jesus had been at the table with his disciples was at the Last Supper, of which this story is highly reminiscent. In any case, it was then, when he broke the bread and gave it to them, that "their eyes were opened, and they recognized him; and he vanished from their sight" (31). It was then that they also recognized that there was something special about his teaching along the road—something special that they described in terms of a "burning" in their hearts (32).

Luke 22:19	Luke 24:30
Then he took a loaf of bread, and when he had given thanks, he broke it and gave it to them.	When . . . he took bread, blessed and broke it, and gave it to them.

The Disciples Bring Astonishing News

At that point, perhaps without even waiting to finish their meal ["that same hour" (33)], the two disciples returned to Jerusalem, to tell the rest what had happened to them. They brought astonishing news, and they themselves were astonished by other news. The eleven and their companions were saying that they had confirmation of the Lord's resurrection, for he had appeared to Peter!

The story ends with the two disciples telling the rest that they too know of the Resurrection, for the Lord "had been made known to them in the breaking of the bread" (35).

> Remember that just before the beginning of the story we are studying, Luke tells us that Peter had found the empty tomb, but not that he had seen the Lord. Thus, without actually telling the story, Luke let us know that Jesus did appear to Peter.

Dimension 3: What Does the Bible Mean to Us?

We are studying one of the accounts in Luke's Gospel that gives witness to the Resurrection. During the rest of the week you will be reading (or have already read) other accounts in the same Gospel that also serve as witnesses to the Resurrection.

The Significance of the Story

As we study this text, there are at least three directions in which we may reflect on it in order to relate it to our own lives: first, the significance of the resurrection of Jesus; second, the significance of Scripture for the life of faith; third, the "breaking of the bread" as a means of recognizing the presence of Jesus among us.

- First, let us look at the significance of the resurrection of Jesus. We often hear that the significance of Jesus' resurrection is that it shows that we too shall be raised. That is important, since it affirms our Christian hope in renewed life after death. However, if that were all, it would mean that Jesus died and was raised only to prove what the Pharisees already believed—that there is a future resurrection.

  When the New Testament speaks of the resurrection of Jesus, it means much more than that. It means that in the death and resurrection of Jesus the promises of God for the end-time have begun to be fulfilled. Because Jesus was raised from the dead, death itself has been overcome. The battle has already been won. We are simply living in

the "mopping up" operations. That is the essential faith of the New Testament. This is the faith by which the early Christians lived and the faith for which the early martyrs died. As Paul would say, "Christ has been raised from the dead, the first fruits of those who have died" (1 Corinthians 15:20).
- Secondly, you may wish to look at the manner in which Jesus used Scripture in this text. We often forget that the main thrust of Scripture is to show us God's plan and that God's plan revolves around the person and the work of Jesus Christ. Scripture teaches us morality, yes. Scripture teaches religion, yes. Scripture teaches history, yes. Above all, Scripture witnesses to Jesus. If we read it only as a book of morality, or of religion, or of history, and do not relate it to the mighty act of salvation of God in Jesus Christ, Jesus could well say to us the same that he said to those two disciples: "Oh, how foolish you are, and how slow of heart to believe all that the prophets have declared!" (25)

Jesus Is Known in the "Breaking of Bread"

We often think that the main obstacle we have in reading Scripture and in applying it to our lives lies in questioning its authority, or in not being able to understand its original setting. These are indeed real problems. *The most important problem most Christians have in dealing with Scripture, however, is that we forget that Scripture points to Jesus Christ and through Jesus to what God intends for us to be.* Apart from that perspective, we misread Scripture and turn it into a questionable book of history, or into a legalistic book of morals and religious practice.
- Thirdly (and this appears to be Luke's main purpose in telling this story) we are to remember that our Lord is known to us "in the breaking of the bread." Notice the parallelism between the story of Jesus breaking bread with his disciples in this text and the similar story in the passage about the Last Supper. For the two disciples, this was like Communion. In that Communion they recognized Jesus. (Later, as we study the Book of Acts, we shall see that the early church continued gathering for "the breaking of the bread.")

We Protestants often forget that throughout most of its history the Christian church has considered Communion its highest and normative act of worship. Only in recent years have we begun to recover the sense of the significance of "the breaking of the bread." Why did the early church find this act so significant?

—Because in breaking bread together they remembered and celebrated Jesus' act of giving his life for them.
—Because in the breaking of the bread they also celebrated Jesus' victory over death, the reason why the story of the disciples at Emmaus is so important.

— Because in the breaking of the bread, they celebrated and pre-enacted the Great Banquet of the end-times, when all of God's people will be brought together from all corners of the earth and all times in history. It is for the same reasons that the breaking of the bread is still so important for us today.
— Because in that act we are united with the suffering and the sacrifice of Christ.
— Because in that very act we are also united with his victory.
— Because in breaking bread together now, in the midst of our common pilgrimage, we pre-enact and we celebrate the coming great feast of the Lord!

Quite often, like those two disciples walking to Emmaus, we are perplexed and puzzled. We have indications that there is reason to hope, just as they did. But there are also powerful forces arrayed against us, which hide Christ's victory from us. In those circumstances, in our own walk through life, we may find that we too shall see him in the breaking of the bread!

Dimension 4:
A Daily Bible Journey Plan

Day 1: Luke 23:26-38

Day 2: Luke 23:39-49

Day 3: Luke 23:50-56

Day 4: Luke 24:1-12

Day 5: Luke 24:13-35

Day 6: Luke 24:36-49

Day 7: Luke 24:50-53

GLOSSARY

Annunciation—[uh-nuhn-see-AY-shuhn] Announcement by the angel Gabriel to Mary that she would give birth to the Son of God by the power of the Holy Spirit (Luke 1:26-38).

Bethany—[BETH-uh-nee] A small town on the Mount of Olives near Jerusalem. The home of Mary, Martha, Lazarus, and Simon the leper (John 11:1-44; Matthew 26:5-13).

Bethel—[BETH-uhl] A town of Palestine, eleven miles north of Jerusalem. Originally called Luz, this town is mentioned more than any other biblical town except Jerusalem.

Bethlehem—[BETH-li-hem] A town in the hill country of Judah, five miles south of Jerusalem. David came from Bethlehem, and it was expected that the Messiah would be born there (Micah 5:2). Joseph and Mary went there to be registered at the time of Jesus' birth.

Calvary—[KAL-vuh-ree] A place located just outside the walls of Jerusalem where Jesus was crucified.

Crucifixion—[kroo-suh-FIX-shuhn] An act of fixing a person to a cross for the purpose of capital punishment. Jesus died in this manner.

Demon—[DEE-muhn] A spirit with minor powers. The New Testament depicts demons as evil spirits exercising malevolent influences.

Disciple—[di-SIGH-puhl] A pupil or follower of a teacher, used especially of the Twelve.

Emmaus—[i-MAY-uhs] A village about seven miles northwest of Jerusalem. Two disciples met Jesus on the road to this town following Jesus' resurrection (Luke 24:13-35).

Galilee—[GAL-uh-lee] The northern region of Palestine. The region was separated from Judea by Samaria. Nazareth, home of Jesus, was in Galilee.

Gentiles—[JEN-tighlz] All people of the world other than the Jews.

Golgotha—[GOL-guh-thuh] The place of a skull. Name of a hill outside the gates of Jerusalem where Jesus was crucified (Matthew 27:32-37).

Gospel—[GOS-puhl] (1) Good news concerning Christ, the kingdom of God, and salvation. (2) One of four books—

Matthew, Mark, Luke, and John—containing the authorized story of the life and teachings of Jesus Christ.

Herod—[HER-uhd] Known as Herod the Great. He ruled Palestine (37-34 B.C.). King at the time of Jesus' birth, he was known for his building projects, including the Temple in Jerusalem.

Herod Antipas—[HER-uhd AN-tee-puhs] He ruled Galilee and Perea (4 B.C.-A.D. 39). Called by Jesus "that fox" (Luke 13:31-32), he had John the Baptist killed. Pilate sent Jesus to him to be tried (Luke 23:6-12).

Jairus—[jay-IGH-ruhs] A ruler of the synagogue, probably in Capernaum. Jesus raised his daughter from the dead (Luke 8:41-56).

Jerusalem—[ji-ROO-suh-luhm] A city located on a tableland on the crest of the central ridge of Palestine. It was the site of the Temple. Known as Zion, it was destroyed by the Babylonians in 587-86 B.C. and again by the Romans in A.D. 70.

Jordan—[JOR-duhn] Means the descender. The most important river of Palestine, it flows over 200 miles from Baniyas in ancient Caesarea Philippi to the southern tip of the Dead Sea.

Judea—[*joo*-DEE-uh] A province in southern Palestine ruled by the Roman procurator. It included the city of Jerusalem.

Luke—[Loo-k] Writer of the books of Luke and Acts.

Messiah—[muh-SIGH-uh] One anointed with holy oil, as a priest or a king. King David became the type of the future Messiah who would deliver his people (Isaiah 9:6-7; 11:1-5). Peter identified Jesus as the Messiah (Matthew 16:13-20).

Nazareth—[NAZ-uh-rith] A town in lower Galilee where Mary and Joseph lived and where Jesus was brought up (Luke 2:39-40). The townspeople rejected Jesus when he announced his mission (Luke 4:16-30).

Pharisees—[FAIR-uh-seez] One of three chief Jewish parties. They strictly adhered to Mosaic law and traditional interpretations of the elders. Jesus denounced them often as self-righteous and hypocritical (Matthew 5:20, 23).

Pontius Pilate—[PON-shuhs PIGH-luht] Roman procurator of Judea (A.D. 26-36). He ordered that Jesus be crucified in spite of the fact that he could not find any evil in him (John 18:28–19:16a).

Publican—[PUHB-li-kuhn] A collector of Roman taxes and customs. The right to be a tax collector was auctioned to the highest bidder. As a group they were unpopular because they increased the tax in order to increase their own fortunes (Luke 3:12-13; 19:8). Matthew and Zacchaeus were publicans.

Sabbath—[SAB-uhth] Seventh day of the week, divinely instituted day of rest (Exodus 20:8-11). The day was strictly observed at the time of Jesus. He viewed the sabbath as being for human benefit (Mark 2:23-28).

Scribes—[skr-eye-bz] Interpreters or teachers of Mosaic law. Scribes came to be addressed with respectful titles, particularly "Rabbi" (my master, my teacher). At the root of the conflict between Jesus and the scribes lay the question of his independent interpretation of the Scriptures.

Sepulchre—[SEP-uhl-kuhr] Caverns, natural or artificial, in which the Jews buried their dead. They were closed by heavy stones to keep out animals (Mark 15:42–16:4).

Synagogue—[SIN-uh-gog] Jewish place of worship, also used as a law court and school. Probably arose during Babylonian captivity when Temple worship was impossible.

Syria—[SIHR-ee-uh] Country on the east coast of the Mediterranean and extending inland, north and east of Israel. Antioch was its capital. Damascus was also in Syria.

Temple—[TEM-puhl] A building dedicated to the worship of God, first built by Solomon in Jerusalem. A second Temple was built following the Exile. Herod's Temple superseded the second Temple and was the Temple at the time of Jesus. This Temple was destroyed by the Romans in A.D. 70.

Theophilus—[thee-OFF-uh-luhs] The person to whom Luke addressed the Gospel (Luke 1:1-3) and Acts (1:1). A man of prominence, his name meant "lover of God."

Zacchaeus—[za-KEE-uhs] Wealthy tax collector from Jericho whose life was changed by an encounter with Jesus (Luke 19:1-10).

Zealots—[ZEL-uhtz] A party of Jews started by Judas the Galilean to resist Roman aggression. Simon the disciple was a member of this group (Luke 6:15).

www.ingramcontent.com/pod-product-compliance
Lightning Source LLC
LaVergne TN
LVHW031630070426
835507LV00024B/3412